How to Do
Own Divorce

How to Do Your Own Divorce

A step-by-step guide

Jeremy Rosenblatt

Vermilion
LONDON

FOR MY MOTHER AND MY FATHER
RUTH AND ELLIOT ROSENBLATT

WITH LOVE

First published in 1993 by Vermilion
an imprint of Ebury Press
Random House
20 Vauxhall Bridge Road
London SW1V 2SA

www.randomhouse.co.uk

Fourth edition revised and updated 2001

The Random House Group Limited Reg. No. 954009

Catalogue record for this book is available
from the British Library.

ISBN 0 09 185739 2

Cover design by Patrick McCreeth
Cover illustration by Christopher Brown

Typeset in Palatino
by SX Composing DTP, Rayleigh, Essex
Printed and bound by Mackays of Chatham PLC, Chatham, Kent

Contents

About the Author

Jeremy Rosenblatt read law at the London School of Economics before working as a Research Assistant at the House of Commons. He is the winner of an Anglo-Dutch Cultural Scholarship to the Asser Institute of International Law in the Hague and a Guggenheim Travel Scholarship to Venice. He is a sometime contributor to television and radio and is a trained psychotherapist. He is the author of *International Adoption* (Sweet and Maxwell) and *International Conventions Affecting Children* (Kluwer Law International), and co-author of *International Child Abduction* (Sweet and Maxwell) and *Children and Immigration* (Cavendish). Jeremy Rosenblatt is a family barrister living and working in London.

Acknowledgements

The enclosed forms are acknowledged as copyright reproduced with the permission of the Controller of Her Majesty's Stationery Office and the Solicitor's Stationery Society.

Pamela Curwen is thanked for her suggestion that there be a chapter entitled 'How to Use this Book'.

The instructing solicitors of Jeremy Rosenblatt are thanked for their invaluable suggestions and their belief, with the author, that those parties who cannot afford representation either privately or by means of the legal aid fund must be assisted alternatively.

How to use this book

This book is primarily written for those who find themselves unable to afford legal representation upon divorce, either through the inability to pay lawyers privately or by reason of their inability to obtain legal aid in its entirety or by even making a contribution towards the legal aid fund. It is also written for those who may decide to represent themselves for whatever reason. For such persons, reading the Introduction is important as it considers the limitations that may arise in representing themselves.

It may be useful to read the book through on a number of occasions. It is likely to be a slow read because until the moment you need *How to Do Your Own Divorce* you have probably been quite unaware of this particular legal process. In addition, you have probably never had to consider how a decision concerning divorce could have a catastrophic effect on the rest of your life. Of course any life change can also bring about positive results and *How to Do Your Own Divorce* tries to set out this unfamiliar procedure as simply as it is possible to make it.

After reading this chapter and the Introduction, read Chapter 4 on Judicial Separation and remind yourself that the procedure can be taken slowly by not immediately seeking a divorce. Chapter 1, Before You Get Divorced, sets out the aspects of the divorce petition itself, which in time will change when the parts of the Family Law Act 1996 dealing with 'No Fault Divorce' come into being. In due course, the procedure will be more straightforward.

Please do remember that, ultimately, systems are supposed to be about pragmatism and common sense, and the procedure for divorce and redistributing the finances in England and Wales exists solely for the purpose of sorting out marital problems when they can no longer be sorted out by the parties alone. However, the system will inevitably hold disappointments for one party or the other, or the two of them. It will not always take into account past bad behaviour that is perceived by the one or the other to be relevant, and may also make decisions that can ignore the concept that one has contributed a little more, financially, to the marriage at the time of divorce or separation. Few walk away from a divorce with pleasure, especially after the redistribution of family finances and of course after a dispute concerning children, because there is little pleasurable about divorce itself. Please absorb as many of these realities as possible as you slowly read the chapters and then perhaps read them again.

As well as being used to assist in representation, this book can also benefit a party who is represented and who begins to understand the system and the process by reading it, whilst the solicitor or barrister continues to represent them.

The Petitioner is referred to in this volume in the feminine. There exists no adverse reason for this.

Introduction

Britain has the highest marriage rate of any country in the EU. It also has the highest proportion of single parents and the highest divorce rate: an astonishing 40 per cent of marriages in Britain end in divorce. The reasons, in descending order of frequency, are:

- money, or the lack of it
- alcohol- and drug-related problems
- extra-marital relationships

Of these, money problems are by far the most common cause of a marriage breaking up. When one or other partner loses their job – a situation that occurs all too often during an economic recession – the couple often find themselves in unexpected financial difficulties. As a consequence, unbearable strains are put on the relationship.

If the partners are owner-occupiers they may not be able to meet their mortgage repayments. But selling up and moving somewhere cheaper is not always possible when the property market is at a low ebb, and the building society may simply have to repossess their home. Without an income, pension contributions will no longer be made, and any capital saved in bank or building society accounts will rapidly dwindle. From a situation of relative comfort the couple may find themselves in the unfamiliar and frightening position of depending on the state for unemployment benefit and Income Support. If there are children the economic strain will be intensified because there are more mouths to feed, and what little money is available has to be stretched even further. It is against this kind of background that people's feelings for one another disintegrate. If the situation becomes serious, the marriage itself is likely to fall apart.

At this stage, divorce is not the only legal option. Judicial separation (formerly known as legal separation: see p.30) enables the partners to be separated in the eyes of the law without actually being divorced.

Divorce is a traumatic time for everyone concerned. The aim of *How to Do Your Own Divorce* is to offer legal assistance to husbands and wives whose marriages have irretrievably broken down, and in particular to show them how to conduct their own divorce in the courts of England and Wales without going to the expense of hiring a lawyer (the law in Scotland is different, and it is not possible to go into the Scottish system in a short book such as this). Intended as a practical guide through the potential minefield of a divorce, this book does not discuss emotional issues: these are amply catered for by a large number of excellent organisations whose names and addresses are listed on p.65.

The different stages of a divorce case are clearly defined, and the legal terminology – which can be baffling and off-putting to the general public – is carefully explained so that the various terms will be familiar when you encounter them in court. The first stage, petitioning for divorce, is quite straightforward. It involves filling out pre-printed forms, then ensuring that the other party receives them, before delivering them to court and going on to the pronouncements of decree nisi and decree absolute. Instructing a solicitor to do this on your behalf might cost about £300, so by doing it yourself you can make a worthwhile saving at what may already be a difficult financial time.

The subsequent stages of a divorce, involving the division of the couple's money and property and the future of any children of the marriage, are unfortunately more complicated. Users of this book might therefore feel confident enough to represent themselves at the beginning but not at the later stages. If, however, you do decide to tackle the financial stages yourself but find the process more complicated than you had realised, contact a solicitor and ask him or her to take over. There is little point in trying to save yourself money if you end up making a bad job of it. Remember, you may be eligible for legal aid (see p.67 for further information on lawyers, costs and legal aid).

Beginning on p.86 you will find samples of a number of legal forms relating to divorce. No one enjoys filling in forms, especially when they are long and full of technicalities. But while some of these documents might appear complex at first, if you read through them carefully you will see that all they want you to do is to give as much detail as possible regarding your particular application. The aim is to help you, the other side and the court – there is no ulterior motive. At the end of the day the more honest you are in filling out these forms and providing the information asked for, the quicker the entire process will be and the sooner you can start getting on with the rest of your life.

Since the second edition of this book the Family Law Act 1996 has been passed. In due course the entire process of divorce will change and the 'No Fault' divorce will finally come into being. The new process will drastically alter the entire procedure outlined in Chapter 1, Before You Decide to Get Divorced, and Chapter 3, From the Petition to Decree Absolute. This new third edition relates to the procedure as it presently remains.

In some courts in England and Wales a pilot scheme was temporarily introduced to develop a fast track procedure for financial resolution. Any future edition of *How to Do Your Own Divorce* will include such a scheme if the procedure becomes a permanent feature of the divorce process.

In addition, as this book goes to print the government is considering introducing pre-nuptial agreements determined by parties as having an element of binding force.

1

Before You Decide to Get Divorced

If you have got to the point where you or your partner, or both of you, feel that your marriage is no longer viable and you want to get divorced, the law allows you to do so under certain conditions laid down by the Matrimonial Causes Act 1973 as amended by the Family Law Act 1996.

After not less than one year of marriage, a petition for divorce – the document that begins the whole process – may be presented to a court by either partner in a marriage that has broken down irretrievably. There are five legally acceptable reasons for a marriage to have reached this stage:

- adultery and unreasonable behaviour
- unacceptable behaviour
- desertion for a continuous two-year period
- two years' continuous separation with the respondent's consent
- five years' continuous separation with or without the respondent's consent

Before a divorce can be considered, you must satisfy the court that at least one of these is true in your case.

Adultery and Unreasonable Behaviour

In legal terms adultery means voluntary sexual intercourse between two members of the opposite sex, one or both of whom are married, though not to each other. If the adultery is admitted it is much easier to prove the grounds for divorce; if it is not, witnesses may be required.

If, after the allegation of adultery, the husband or wife resume living together for a period of six months in total, the adultery will not be regarded as a ground for divorce (this is called the six-month cohabitation rule). It does not matter how long ago the adultery took place as long as the parties have not gone back to live with each other for six months altogether.

But it is not enough just to satisfy these conditions and prove adultery. The petitioner (the person bringing the petition for divorce) must also show that to continue living with the respondent (the partner on whom the petition is served) would create an intolerable situation. The test is a subjective one: it might not be intolerable for everybody, but as long as the petitioner states it is intolerable, that is enough. Nor does the state of intolerability have to stem from the proven adultery – it might arise from a whole host of other things.

Unreasonable Behaviour

In legal terms, this means that the respondent has behaved in such a way that the petitioner cannot reasonably be expected to live with the respondent. Examples of such behaviour patterns include:

- physical violence
- alcohol or drug abuse
- psychological distress
- growing apart
- arguments
- lack of, or too much, sexual intercourse

The six-month cohabitation rule (see above) applies here too.

Desertion

This means that the respondent has left the petitioner for a continuous period of at least two years immediately before the presentation of the petition. No allegation of misconduct is necessary for a divorce to be granted on grounds of desertion, but the court does have to be satisfied on four matters:

- The fact of separation. It may be enough for the parties still to occupy the same home if they live separately within it

and do not communicate with each other
- An intention to desert (one partner leaves the other, with no intention of returning), which in itself brings the cohabitation to its end
- That separation was without consent. (The fact that the deserted partner is delighted will not unduly affect the concept of desertion as a ground for divorce)
- That one partner did not have a good reason for living apart from the other, such as needing to take a job in another country

Any period of cohabitation cannot be included in the two-year desertion period – it has to be consistently uninterrupted.

Two Years' Separation and Respondent's Consent

The husband and wife must have lived apart for a continuous period of at least two years immediately before the presentation of the petition, and the respondent must consent to a decree being granted. Again, there need be no allegation of misconduct. The parties can still live under the same roof as long as they are not living as 'husband and wife'.

Either the husband or the wife must have considered the marriage to be at its end throughout the two-year separation period. The partner who is relying on this ground must state the date when this conclusion was reached, and the circumstances. The respondent must give his or her signed consent regarding the fact of separation relied upon by the petitioner.

Five Years' Separation

The husband and wife must have lived apart for a continuous period of at least five years immediately before the presentation of the petition. The respondent's consent is unnecessary.

In legal terminology, the consistency of the separation period and the consideration by one party that the marriage was at its end must be shown. In other words, one of the partners can suggest when it ended and the other can agree; if they do not agree, the divorce might be defended on this issue.

There is also a special defence which can be used against the ground of five years' separation. If the respondent can claim that the divorce would cause him or her grave financial or other hardship, the petition can be opposed. The hardship must be shown to be a consequence of the actual dissolution of the marriage, and not just of its breakdown.

Reconciliation and Therapy

The British are reluctant to look too closely at themselves as individuals because this is regarded as unhealthy self-obsession. In Catholic countries people tend to be more open emotionally and they have the additional outlet of confession to a priest, while America abounds with therapists of all kinds and no one need ever keep their problems to themselves. But on the whole the British have no such safety valve, and traditional social values demand that we keep a stiff upper lip and suffer in silence. Unfortunately, this situation only serves to create an atmosphere of simmering tension which may at some stage boil over, possibly into a demand for divorce.

One reason why a marriage might not be working is that one partner has a problem which he or she has not addressed or even necessarily identified. During the course of a marriage problems originating in childhood may surface and reveal themselves in the shape of, say, alcoholism or drug abuse. The argument that such addictions have become evident because of the other partner's attitude does not always hold water. Often these behaviour traits have been there in some form all the time, irrespective of the existence of the partner or of the marriage itself. In such a situation the partner with the problem should make every effort to seek professional help, rather than destroy the marriage because of something within himself or herself as an individual.

Much weight is attached by the courts to what is known as reconciliation between the parties prior to divorce, and while that is to be applauded, not enough consideration is given to the needs of the individual alone as opposed to those of the husband and wife together. Such needs can be met by therapy in all forms from straightforward counselling to psycho-therapy. To help you choose the therapy that best suits your needs you could discuss the matter with your GP in the first instance. Notice boards in court waiting areas advertise a range of therapy centres, and the organisations listed on p.65 may also be of assistance.

Only when you have taken steps to deal with any problems within yourself as an individual should you consider attempt-ing the next stage – reconciliation to the potential divorce between the two parties.

Reconciliation Before Divorce

If both parties are going to be legally represented, what is called a certificate of reconciliation should be filed at the court along with the divorce petition. This certificate states whether you have received advice about reconciliation.

During the preliminary stages of the hearing you can have what are called conciliation appointments at court, when you can ask questions of a conciliation officer appointed by the court. Often relationships are saved and marriages remain intact all because of a thirty-minute session which allows the officer to mediate and prevent a couple's anger running out of control.

Where lengthier conciliation is thought appropriate, organ-isations such as RELATE (formerly the Marriage Guidance Council) provide excellent services to enable the husband and wife to sift through the main areas of disagreement. The court system is experienced at pointing people in the right direction for advice of this kind.

Before considering the legal procedure of petitioning for divorce, the steps described above must be given due atten-tion – which means more than mere lip-service.

Mediation

At present the Family Law Act 1996 Part III (26) provides Legal Aid for mediation in family matters and (27) provides the provision and availability of mediation; (28) provides payment for mediation; (29) provides payment for mediation and legal aid. In due course mediation might be a compulsory part of the divorce process.

Your Legal Rights

When you or your children have been the victim of domestic cruelty of one kind or another, you may want to throw your partner out of the family home. But until you are divorced you have no automatic legal right to do so. If you change the locks, for instance, your partner can obtain a court order enabling him to get back into the home. What you must do in this situation is go to the court to obtain an injunction, known as an exclusion order, to prevent him from entering; only then are you at liberty to change the locks.

If you have suffered anything from harassment to actual violence you may want to obtain a non-molestation injunction. The purpose of this kind of injunction, also known as a personal protection order, is to stop your partner interfering with you or your children. If you have not yet initiated divorce proceedings, you apply to the magistrates' court for a non-molestation injunction; if you have set the ball rolling, or are about to, the divorce court can give you a personal protection order. In the event that your partner fails to comply with either of these two injunctions he can be sent to prison.

The list of organisations on p.65 includes several which can help in such circumstances.

2

Maintenance Before Divorce Proceedings Are Begun

Money is involved at all stages in a divorce. For simplicity, it can be divided into:

- maintenance before divorce proceedings are initiated (which is what this chapter is about)
- the costs of the actual divorce (see p. 28)
- maintenance arrangements while the divorce is going on, which is known as maintenance pending suit (see Chapter 5)
- the division of the divorcing couple's assets (see Chapter 6)
- permanent maintenance arrangements (see Chapter 6)

Maintenance Orders

Before you petition for either divorce or a judicial separation, you can apply to the family proceedings court (formerly magistrates' court) for an order for financial provision if your partner is not supporting you properly. The Domestic Proceedings and Magistrates' Courts Act 1978 allows either party of the marriage to seek an order where there has been:

- failure to provide reasonable maintenance. The court will consider the wife's needs, obligations and responsibilities in relation to her income, earning capacity and resources, as well as the husband's ability to pay. The wife should show that the husband has been difficult about making money available – for instance that he has made only a few payments or none at all, or that, while pleading impoverishment, he has been seen eating in expensive restaurants and has gone on holiday

- unreasonable behaviour. The court will consider whether the husband has behaved in such a way (drunkenness, say, or physical violence) that it would be unreasonable to expect the wife to continue living with him
- desertion by the husband of the wife who is applying for the order. After hearing what the wife has to say, the court will consider whether desertion can be proved sufficiently as a ground to bring the money application

If the ground is proven, the court can go on to order either periodical payments or a lump sum payment to the wife. There is a limit on what the family proceedings court can award. However, a consent order, which is based on an agreement between the two partners, has no ceiling.

A periodical payments order can be made under section 7 of the Domestic Proceedings and Magistrates' Court Act 1978:

- if the parties have been living continuously apart for more than three months though not in a state of desertion, or
- if the other party has been making periodical payments to the applicant

The applicant should specify the total amount of money already received in the three months before she made the application. If the amount ordered would have been less under section 2 of the Act, then the court must order an amount at that level and not under section 7. Once more the court will consider the needs of the parties, the standard of living enjoyed before separation and so on.

An order cannot be backdated to before the date of the application (though a lump sum order can be made to augment the maintenance money), nor can it go on beyond the death of either party. (If the two parties subsequently divorce, the order will come to its end if the party receiving payment remarries.)

Under section 19 of the Act an interim maintenance order can be made. It remains in force for three months, but can be renewed for another three months; it will cease when a final order is made. It is not possible to appeal against an interim order.

How to Apply

The family proceedings court has jurisdiction if at the time of the application:

- both parties reside in England or Wales, or
- the respondent resides in Scotland or Northern Ireland and the parties last resided as man and wife in England or Wales

The court can hear an application to revoke or vary an order (see p.21) even though one party resides outside England or Wales. The application should be made in the court covering the area where the parties last resided.

Applications, whether for ordinary periodical payments or for a consent order, should be made on standard court forms. State the grounds upon which the application is based – that the family needs money because there is insufficient income coming in and the father, for example, can well afford to make a reasonable payment.

Once the court receives the application it will notify the respondent. The Clerk of the Justices usually decides what evidence is to be heard and when; the applicant should simply follow his instructions.

The court will ask for a statement of means, giving full details of the financial circumstances of the applicant. The kind of documentary evidence required in court includes such things as:

- pay slips
- P60s
- bank or post office statements
- quarterly bills

This evidence should be shown to the respondent before the couple come to court.

At the hearing, which both applicant and respondent are required to attend, the applicant simply confirms the contents of the financial statement as true, adding anything that has not already been detailed and formally exhibited to the court (called 'handed up to the court').

The applicant will then be cross-examined by the respondent or his legal representative, and the Clerk of the Justices might also have some questions. If the applicant has brought any witnesses who are relevant to her financial situation, they will be called after the applicant's evidence has been given. Then the respondent will give his evidence in reply and the applicant can ask him questions, guided by the Clerk if necessary.

Variation of Orders (see p. 82)

Orders made under sections 2, 6 or 7 of the Domestic Proceedings and Magistrates' Courts Act 1978 can be varied or even revoked by a family proceedings court. Orders for periodical payments and interim orders can be revoked as well. The court can order a lump sum to be paid as a means of varying an order of periodical payments.

In this situation the court will inevitably consider any agreement reached between the parties, as well as the circumstances of the case. Either of the two parties may apply for a variation of the order.

3

From Petition to Decree Absolute

A court in England or Wales (though Scotland and Northern Ireland are different) can grant a decree of:

- divorce
- nullity, or
- separation

These are legal choices available to the divorcing couple for formalising the end of a marriage.

Nullity means that the marriage is ruled never to have been in existence – as, for example, when one partner was pressured into marrying the other. Judicial separation, which some couples use as a 'cooling-off period' while they are deciding whether to get divorced, is dealt with in Chapter 4. Meanwhile this chapter gives a step-by-step account of how to obtain a divorce. Financial arrangements during divorce proceedings are discussed in Chapter 5, while information on maintenance after divorce will be found in Chapter 6.

Preparing and Filing the Petition

To initiate divorce proceedings, whichever partner is seeking the divorce (the petitioner) files a petition. This simply means sending two copies of the divorce application to any county court with divorce jurisdiction (see p.77), or to the Divorce Registry in London. The petition must use standard wording and be presented in a particular way (see p.86). Forms for this purpose are available from divorce court offices or the Divorce Registry.

A third copy of the petition is required if the reason for divorce is adultery with a named co-respondent. The petitioner must name the co-respondent if an allegation of adultery is being relied upon as the ground for divorce, unless the name and identity of the person involved are unknown; in this situation the petition must state that they are unknown.

Sometimes the petitioner believes that no actual act of adultery has been committed, but wishes to rely for grounds of divorce on what is known as an improper association. This means that the respondent and the third party might, for instance, have had regular intimate dinners together, though never a sexual relationship. In this case the petitioner must make a special application for the court to direct whether this person should become a co-respondent. The application should be made at the directions hearing (see p.27).

Even if both parties agree to the divorce, it is not possible to file a joint petition – you must decide between yourselves which of you will be cast as petitioner and which as respondent. Your choice of role in this situation is purely a formality and does not usually have any bearing on how the court subsequently deals with children and financial matters.

At the date of the petition, one or other of the parties must have been permanently and consistently resident in England or Wales for a period of one year.

Various other documents must be filed at court at the same time. Briefly (and with certain exceptions), these are:

- marriage certificate
- statement of arrangements for children
- certificate of reconciliation
- a fee is also payable

First, the marriage certificate: if the original is not available (and remember, it will not be returned afterwards), an official copy can be obtained from the General Registry of Births, Deaths and Marriages, OPCS Southport, Smedley Hydro, Trafalgar Road, Birkdale, Southport, Merseyside, or from the General Register Office, St Catherine's House, Kingsway, London WC2B 6JP. An ordinary photocopy is not acceptable, and if the certificate is in another language it must be accompanied by an authenticated translation.

You must also present two copies of a completed form (available from the same sources as the petition form) stating what arrangements are proposed for any children of the two parties. 'Children' in this context (called 'relevant children' on the form) means young people under sixteen, or under eighteen and still undergoing full-time education or training, who are:

- blood children of either the husband or the wife
- legally adopted children
- stepchildren
- any other children if one of the divorcing partners believes that they were brought up by one or other of them within the family itself

Children are often the casualties of divorce, and their interests are therefore rightly regarded by the court as being of paramount importance. The court will want to know about practical arrangements once the divorce is complete: where the children will live, with whom, whether the other parent will be in contact and the frequency of that contact, schooling, general day-to-day care and maintenance. If the divorcing parents cannot agree which of them the child should live with (residency), decree absolute will not be pronounced until this matter is resolved (see Chapter 7).

At this early stage it may not be possible to answer all the questions on the statement of arrangements form, so just give answers where you can. Any previous orders relating to the children or any information to do with the marriage (living abroad, for instance, or the children going to school in another country) should accompany the petition.

If, when the respondent receives his copy of the divorce petition and the accompanying documents, he agrees with the proposed arrangements for the children, he should sign the statement of arrangements form. Alternatively, he can send his own proposals to the court on a form and the court will send a copy to the petitioner.

If the district judge is satisfied with the statement of arrangements for the children, the petitioner will receive a form stating that the court will not have to exercise its powers under the Children Act 1989. However, if the judge is not satisfied, the matter will have to go to trial (see Chapter 7).

As mentioned earlier, a divorcing husband or wife acting on his or her own behalf and not employing a solicitor does not have to include with the petition a certificate of reconciliation (see p.16). However, it is always sensible to consider the possibility of reconciliation before filing for divorce.

The last page of the petition, known as the prayer, is actually a request to the court for:

- the marriage to be dissolved
- an order for costs (that is, of the divorce itself) to be made against the respondent and/or the co-respondent (there is no obligation to follow this through if for any reason you change your mind)
- ancillary relief (a general application for maintenance). Remember to claim this now, or you may be barred from doing so later in the proceedings
- any orders in relation to the children

The petition asks for your solicitor's signature. Obviously, if you are conducting your own case you will sign it yourself. A fee is payable when the petition is filed. This is waived if the petitioner is in receipt of Income Support or Working Families Tax Credit, or is participating in what is known as the green form scheme for those on low incomes (see p.68).

Serving the Petition

Once all these documents have been received by the court, it forwards to the respondent one copy of the petition and one copy of the statement of arrangements for children. Accompanying them are a notice of proceedings and an acknowledgement form; the respondent should sign the latter and return it to the court as proof of service. Where adultery is alleged and the co-respondent has been named on the petition, a copy of the petition and an acknowledgement form are also sent to that person.

What are known as copies of service should be obtained by the court for all parties to the divorce. A copy of service is documentary proof that the other side has been sent the petition: a recorded delivery receipt, for example, would do.

If the acknowledgement of service form is not returned to the court and the postman has been unable to deliver the documents, the court resorts to personal service. This means that the documents are delivered personally by the bailiff of the county court or a process server; the petitioner will probably have to pay for this. Both bailiff and process server have to provide the court with an affidavit that the respondent or co-respondent has indeed received the documents. (If you wish to save money, it is in fact quite acceptable for anyone over the age of sixteen to carry out personal service of documents, and then to complete an affidavit to say that they have done so.)

Personal service is sometimes necessary where the respondent or co-respondent is trying to avoid receiving the documents and is therefore unlikely to sign for recorded delivery. Where service cannot be achieved, an order for 'substituted service' can be sought: this means that the court will be satisfied by an advertisement in a newspaper, for example.

Undefended Petition

When the respondent receives his copy of the petition, he is invited to show notice of intention to defend the divorce. If he does not do so, or if he does not file an answer which states what he feels about the petition (see p.89), then the matter will go ahead as an undefended divorce. This is the most common kind. (Defended divorces are discussed on p.29.)

The petitioner must now swear an affidavit supporting her grounds of divorce. It is filed with the application for the next stage, which is called directions for trial.

There are five standard types of affidavit to choose from, depending upon the ground of divorce relied upon, and the forms can be obtained from the divorce court counter. The petitioner should state quite simply what has happened to bring about the seeking of a divorce.

The petitioner must always identify the signature of the respondent if the acknowledgement of service is signed in order to prove service, and this should be attached to the affidavit in support. If the respondent is making admissions relied upon by the petitioner and/or consenting to the divorce he too must sign, making those admissions and/or giving his consent. In matters of adultery, the co-respondent must do likewise.

The petitioner can then apply at the court divorce counter for a directions hearing. This is a hearing before a district judge at which he can order any further information he thinks should be presented. The district judge's aim here is to assist the final hearing; for instance, he may issue directions to file evidence in affidavit form within a certain time, so that by the date of the final hearing all the evidence will be available.

If the divorce is thought to be an ordinary one without complications, as most are, it will be put on what is called a special procedure list. An application for directions for trial (see below) and an affidavit of evidence, which must be sworn in front of a witnessing person (there will be someone at the court counter), should be made.

The affidavit must state:

- that the respondent (and co-respondent, where appropriate) have received the petition
- that the respondent and any named person admit to adultery (or else whatever other ground of divorce is relied upon)
- that the respondent consents to divorce where the grounds are living apart for two years and the arrangements for the children are agreed to

Directions for Trial

At this stage, which the petitioner does not have to attend, the district judge considers the petition, the affidavit in support and other documents that are being relied upon. He will then state either his satisfaction or dissatisfaction that the petitioner is entitled to the decree.

Dissatisfaction usually arises where the proper procedures have not been followed or where certain admissions that are required by the court have not been forthcoming. In this event the case may be withdrawn from the special procedure list, or the petitioner may be given a further opportunity to satisfy the court about these grey areas.

Decree Nisi

Once the court is satisfied, a date and time for the pronouncement of a decree nisi by a judge in open court will be supplied. The petitioner, respondent and co-respondent will receive from the court a certificate of entitlement to the decree. Once more, there is no requirement to attend. If there are no children, documentary confirmation will be supplied by the court to the effect that this is indeed so.

Costs

If, in the prayer that forms part of the petition (see p.25), the petitioner has asked for an order for costs to be made against the respondent and/or co-respondent, the court will now consider this matter, which is entirely at its discretion. If the court consents, the petitioner will be sent a form (referred to as supplementary to decree nisi). Copies will also be sent to the respondent and co-respondent as appropriate.

Decree Absolute

The decree absolute may be delayed if the court is not yet satisfied with the arrangements to be made concerning the children. Therefore the petitioner should make sure that she has received from the court a copy of the document which states that the judge has decided that decree absolute need not be held up for this reason. Once this has been received (or if there are no children) the petitioner can apply for decree absolute, using yet another standard form and paying a fee to the court office, as soon as six weeks have elapsed since the decree nisi was pronounced.

Unless, as mentioned earlier, the petitioner is exempt from paying fees because she is receiving state benefit, a fee is payable when you apply for decree absolute. Copies of the decree absolute, which must be produced if either of the divorcing partners wishes to get married again, will then be sent by the court to the petitioner, the respondent and, where relevant, the co-respondent.

If there is a delay of more than twelve months between the pronouncing of the decree nisi and the application for decree absolute, a written explanation will be required by the court.

Defended Divorces

Most divorces are not defended – understandably, since defence involves a full hearing in court with all the attendant expense of lawyers. People tend to defend petitions if they feel aggrieved about the way the marriage is coming to its end: often the respondent accepts, albeit grudgingly, that the marriage is over but objects to the reasons stated in the petition.

This does not, however, necessarily justify defending a divorce. A divorce should only be defended where the respondent does not believe that the marriage should end. Even so, bear in mind that in a secular, democratic society it is unlikely that any court is going to make a petitioner remain in a marriage which she believes to be finished.

If you are a respondent and you wish to defend the divorce, you must say so on the notice of proceedings form, which you will receive from the court along with your copy of the petition. This form must be sent back to the court within eight days of your receiving it.

From the date when you receive the petition you have twenty-nine days to file what is known as an answer to the petition (see p.88) – a refutation of the 'facts' of the petition. If no answer is sent to the court within this period, the petitioner can apply for directions for a trial.

The petitioner will herself have to refute whatever defence the respondent makes out, within fourteen days of receiving his answer; this is known as the reply (see p.89). If she simply wants a divorce as quickly as possible, she might feel there is little point in replying as it will waste more time and increase costs. However, as the trial will consider what the respondent has to say in his answer to the petition, the petitioner may have no choice but to refute what he is alleging in defence.

At the hearing in court, which must be attended by both husband and wife, by their legal representatives if any, and by any witnesses, each side will give evidence. The court then makes its finding, either allowing or disallowing the divorce.

4

Judicial Separation

Judicial separation, as opposed to divorce, is sought for one of two reasons:

- the partners want a stepping stone leading up to a petition for divorce. It is often used where a married couple are still uncertain whether they want the finality of divorce, and so they try a period of official separation instead
- the partners acknowledge that the marriage has broken down, but they cannot divorce for religious reasons

The following are exactly the same as in divorce:

- the grounds relied upon
- the timing of a petition – it cannot be brought sooner than one year after the date of marriage
- financial relief
- the obtaining of non-molestation orders and exclusion injunctions in the case of domestic violence
- being judicially separated removes any legal obligation to carry on living with a spouse

But unlike in divorce, neither party can be said to have deserted the other. And where wills are concerned, it is as though the marriage was still in force: if one party dies without making a will, the other will inherit a portion of the estate.

Deed of Separation

This is a document which is normally drawn up privately in a solicitor's office. Since deeds of separation can be complicated it is probably best not to attempt to do this yourself. The document will state the grounds for separation and any arrangements in connection with children, maintenance and expenses. Although the deed is drawn up privately, either party can rely upon it at a later stage if one of them is not complying with its terms – concerning maintenance payments, for example – and they have to go to court.

How to Obtain a Judicial Separation

Getting a judicial separation involves practically the same steps as getting a divorce. As long as the petition passes through undefended, it will appear before the district judge on his special procedure list.

Conciliation features in cases of judicial separation too. It is advisable for the petitioner to make the court aware that conciliation has been considered.

Once the ground is proved, the court grants the decree. Where there are relevant children (see p.24 for a definition), their position has to be clarified by the court before any decree is granted. A decree of judicial separation will not prevent any subsequent divorce being granted on the same facts.

If one partner objects there will be a trial hearing, which will consist of each side saying its piece and the court then making a decision whether or not to grant the separation. In the main the court is likely to grant the separation.

Unlike in divorce, judicial separation comes into being as soon as it is granted – in other words, there is only one decree. Once you are judicially separated, neither of you can marry again unless and until you get divorced.

Financial Matters

Under a judicial separation you can obtain the same financial provision as if you are divorced (see Chapter 6). If you go on to get divorced and seek financial provision there too, you do not necessarily have to gather and produce any more evidence than you will have already gathered as part of the financial hearing on judicial separation.

A husband can still claim the married man's tax allowance even though he is judicially separated. The Inland Revenue rules state that to do so a husband has to live with his wife or at least wholly maintain her. However, the Revenue is fortunately pragmatic and does not usually enforce this rule too rigidly. Of course, spouses often prefer payments to be registered as part of court orders in case payments are not made and then the partner who is paying denies having made any earlier payments. Registration ensures legal recognition and therefore a certain degree of protection.

When a decree of judicial separation is granted, the court may make one of the following financial orders:

- an order that either party shall make to the other such periodical payments, and for such term, as may be specified in the order
- an order that either party shall make to the other, to the satisfaction of the court, such periodical payments, and for such term, as may be specified
- an order that either party shall pay to the other such lump sum or sums as may be specified
- one partner to pay a lump sum to the other, to enable the other to meet liabilities or expenses reasonably incurred in maintaining himself or herself, before making an application for an order in his or her favour
- the payment of a lump sum, or of instalments in amounts specified in the order; the court may require security against the payment of these instalments

Where a decree nisi had been granted based upon two or five years' separation the court can consider the respondent's financial position as it will be after a divorce. The court cannot make a decree absolute unless it is satisfied that the petitioner will not be expected to make any financial payment to the respondent, or that the financial payment which has been made is reasonable, fair or what is called 'the best that can be made altogether'.

The court will expect either provision to be made before the granting of decree absolute, or an undertaking and suggested plan on the part of the petitioner.

Where a couple are judicially separated the court cannot make financial or property adjustment orders unless the respondent has applied for them. However, because the court can withhold decree absolute the petitioner is likely to be sensible regarding the disposition of financial assets.

5

Maintenance During Divorce Proceedings

Because the main financial settlement of a divorce is not made until the decree nisi and does not apply until decree absolute, the courts allow you to claim what is called maintenance pending suit (MPS). This refers to periodical payments which can be made to either the petitioner or the respondent, under section S22 of the Matrimonial Causes Act 1973 as amended by the Family Law Act 1996, while the divorce is going on. Children can also receive periodical payments in their own right at this stage under section S23 of the Act.

MPS can be sought at any time after the presentation of the petition, but do so as soon as possible, as it may take several weeks for the district judge to consider the application and grant any order (though the order can be backdated to the time when the petition was filed). The amount awarded is based on the needs of the person seeking the relief balanced against the ability of the other partner to pay. To obtain an MPS order:

- obtain an application form from the court office
- from the same source, get an affidavit form, on which you will state your means and needs, supported by appropriate bills, pay slips and so on
- at a directions hearing the district judge will issue directions about the evidence required
- the other side has to be served with the application, and in response must swear an affidavit declaring his means and needs. If he fails to do so, the judge will force his hand by setting a high amount for the maintenance order

Periodical payments can be paid either weekly or monthly. An MPS order usually terminates when the decree is made absolute – at which time other, long-term means of financial support will be put into effect.

6

Redistributing the Family Finances

Initiating the Long-term Financial Settlement

As advised in Chapter 2, the application for what is known as ancillary relief is best made in the petition that starts off the whole proceedings (though it is only the petitioner and not the respondent who can do this – see below). Having done so, you should then obtain from the court office the appropriate forms to indicate your intention to proceed with the financial application (they are different for petitioner and respondent). Because of waiting lists in county courts, the notice of application should be filed as soon as possible.

If the application for financial ancillary relief was not made in the petition, leave will have to be granted by the district judge before you can proceed. Leave can be applied for when you give notice that you intend to proceed with the financial application, and the court will then allocate a time for the hearing. Notice of the application must be served on the other side; ordinary post is sufficient for this.

It is sensible for both petitioner and respondent to make any application for financial relief before they receive a decree absolute. No application can be considered if you remarry.

A claim for periodical payments – that is, maintenance money – should also have been made in the petition, as mentioned on p.18. Periodical payment orders can be backdated to when the petition was filed. They can be given a time limit (though an extension can be applied for) and will in any case cease when the payee dies or remarries. A change in the amount can also be applied for (see p.21).

Preliminary Hearings: the First Appointment

The first part of the financial ancillary relief process is the First Appointment. For the First Appointment both parties should prepare a Chronology setting out important dates, such as the date of the marriage, separation and decree nisi if it has taken place, as well as the dates of birth of any children. In addition, a document known as a Statement of Issues should be prepared. This simply sets out the issues between the parties, such as the division of the former matrimonial home, why one party should get more money than the other party, whether the existence of children and their ages should have a particular impact upon the division and whether pensions should be split.

In addition, a Questionnaire, known as a Rule 2.63 Questionnaire, should be drafted setting out questions about the finances of the other party, such as whether the other party has disclosed all bank accounts, whether certain accounts have been deliberately omitted, and what certain transactions within those accounts are actually for if they appear suspicious. The entire purpose of such documentation is to ensure there has been as much preparation as possible and so to shorten any hearing that takes place.

At the First Appointment the district judge will consider the Statement of Issues and clarify whether the questions in the Questionnaire are appropriate, because sometimes unnecessary questions are asked. However, some questions will be essential, even if the other side does not want to have to answer them and claims not to be able to obtain documentation. It must not be forgotten that concealment of anything will be held against the party so concealing. Even if questions are not asked, voluntary disclosure of documents is essential. When further documentation has been delivered to the parties, a Financial Dispute Resolution will be listed.

The Financial Dispute Resolution

The Financial Dispute Resolution is the stage at which a district judge, who will not be the final judge if there is to be a final hearing, will give his opinion during discussion with the parties and their representatives, if they are represented, as to how the assets of the divorce should be divided. Sometimes this opinion is not to the liking of either party, and it may on occasion prompt both parties to reconsider their respective positions and come to a settlement, as settlements save costs. At other times, however, even in the face of the realism of a judge, parties remain reluctant to conciliate. Of course, in reality division is a grey area, and equally so at a final hearing, where the judge has a wide discretion under statute and case law to consider the needs and entitlement of the parties. Following the recent case of White v. White, the judge also has to take into account the equality of the division of the assets. Equal division where affordable is not an absolute but it must be considered.

Directions

At any time during the proceedings the district judge can make directions about the filing and serving of documents.

A date for a directions hearing will be set by the court. Directions are usually no more than plain instructions on what do do next, or on what is expected regarding the transfer of documentary eidence between the parties.

The Family Home and Other Property

In your notice of application and Statement of Issues you should state what you propose should happen to the former family home. Most petitioners want to have the home transferred into their sole name under what is called a property adjustment order. If it is already in your sole name, the other party may contest this.

Where the property adjustment concerns land, you should state:

- where the land is
- whether the title is a registered one; if so, give the title number (your local Land Registry office, whose address can be obtained from the town hall, will give you the title number)
- whether there is a mortgage attached to it

If the petitioner is seeking a property adjustment order, a

copy of the notice of application form must be served on any mortgagee before the district judge will consider the application. Simply write to the building society or bank that is lending the money, advising them of your proposal either to take over the mortgage repayments, if that is the case, or to transfer the house to the petitioner. Their agreement is essential (on this topic, see also Chapter 8).

Stating Your Means to the Court

A Form E is required at this stage, stating the petitioner's financial position in as simple and straightforward a way as possible. It can detail the financial history of the marriage, though what the divorcing couple often do not realise is that, in the main, there is no 'his' or 'hers' or even 'mine' in a marriage; it is all 'ours', and that is why a court has to make the divisions of property unless agreement is reached between the parties themselves.

Form E includes questions on most financial aspects of a marriage, such as mortgage repayments, cars owned, savings, stocks and shares, pension funds, and outgoings in terms of electricity, gas, telephone, water and council tax bills.

Two copies of the notice of application, together with the Form E, must be filed with the court. A fee is payable. The application is officially stamped (this is called sealing) and returned to the petitioner, who must forward it to the respondent, along with a copy of the Form E, within four days. The respondent is required to file a Form E in reply within fourteen days.

More often than not, the petitioner has to apply for a hearing because the two parties cannot agree on the division of assets.

Speeding Up a Slow Respondent

If the respondent does not file a Form E in reply within fourteen days of being served with the notice of application, the petitioner can seek an order from the court that he should do so. If that also fails, the petitioner should go back to court to obtain a further order together with a penal notice (this simply means that if the respondent fails to comply he could be sent to prison unless he can give a good reason for his inaction), and the petitioner should deliver the new documents by personal service (see p.25).

Courts sometimes use interim orders (see pp.20 and 21) as a means of making the respondent comply. If the sum set is very high, the respondent will usually file an affidavit – if only to try to prevent the court setting an even higher sum at the main hearing.

Documents and Evidence Required

All documents relating to financial matters must be produced as evidence of means as has been said above. These would include, where relevant:

- bank statements
- share certificates
- pension policies
- an official valuation of the former family home (normally carried out by an estate agent)

Bank statements usually need to go back to one year before the hearing. Both husband and wife will want to check up on transactions in and out of an account to see if there is anything suspicious. Cash withdrawals, for instance, might indicate that one of the partners is giving someone else money whilst claiming to be impoverished. Cash deposits could mean that one of them has an undisclosed source of income.

Full details of pension policies must be revealed because a petitioning wife, for example, will lose her former husband's pension entitlement once they are divorced. Computations should be obtained from the pension fund managers stating what lump sum and/or income payment the husband would receive on retirement, and what lump sum and/or income payment the wife would have received on the husband's death or on his early retirement.

As the home is often the main asset of the divorcing couple, it is essential that both of them should agree on what it is worth. If they cannot agree, at the directions hearing the district judge may ask for one or two valuers to come to court as witnesses, so that he can then choose an appropriate figure. This, obviously, costs money, so it is always best if the couple can agree the property valuation between them.

Sometimes a witness may be called on to confirm what the divorcing couple say about their financial situation. Ideally, their evidence should first be produced in affidavit form in advance of the hearing if the district judge agrees at the Financial Dispute Resolution. (see under Hearing, p.41).

Showing the Documents to the Other Side

What is known in legal terms as 'discovery of documents' or 'inspection on discovery' (which simply means showing all the documents to the other side) usually takes place fourteen days after the filing of the last affidavit. However, it is sometimes inevitable that certain items, such as the valuation of a home, are not produced until the last minute. Do not be put off if the new evidence is difficult to weigh up immediately. If it is served just before a hearing you can apply for an adjournment. The other side can then be ordered to pay your costs if the fault is thought to be theirs.

Forcing the Other Side's Hand

As mentioned on p.35 before the hearing you can obtain from the court office a copy of a form known as a Rule 2.63 Questionnaire, and use it to ask the respondent whatever you like about financial matters. If, for instance, you want sight of a particular bank statement or share certificate that has not been shown 'on discovery', simply use the form to ask for it to be produced.

If the questions are not answered, an application for directions should be made so that the district judge can order the disclosure of the information concerned. Once more, in this situation a costs order is likely to be made against the unhelpful respondent.

If a particular witness is required – for example, the respondent's high-earning live-in girlfriend – and the respondent refuses to bring her to court, the petitioner can request her to be summonsed through the ordinary court channels. The counter staff will tell you how to go about this. A subpoena form (a legal requirement to appear in court, willingly or not) can then be sent to the other side. Ordinary post can be used in the first instance; if this fails to produce results, use personal service.

The Court Bundle

This is simply the way the court refers to the sheaf of documents which are being used as evidence – bank statements, share certificates, valuations and so on. The bundle should be provided by the applicant for ancillary relief, and its contents must be agreed in advance between petitioner and respondent. Only original documents are permissible. For reference purposes, husband and wife should each take photocopies of all documents for themselves.

The bundle should be limited to essential documents that either party will need to rely upon in the course of giving evidence, or that have already been referred to in affidavits or questionnaires. The court will not want to cope with a massive bundle unless it is strictly necessary.

If the respondent does not agree to certain documents forming part of the bundle, there will have to be two separate bundles, one from the petitioner and the other from the respondent. Once more, this kind of thing takes up extra court time and should be avoided if possible.

The Whole Truth and Nothing but the Truth

When making financial arrangements after divorce, full and frank disclosure is essential as has been reinforced. If one partner conceals money or other assets and this is subsequently discovered, a court will come down strongly on him or her when making its order. Similarly, if one former partner finds out years later that the other failed to disclose a sizeable figure, there is nothing to stop the aggrieved party seeking to set aside an earlier, less generous order. In being honest, divorcing couples are assisting the court and, more importantly, themselves.

The Final Hearing

Before the hearing, both parties must supply a skeleton argument: that is, a written, legal argument setting out what each wants and why. This is disclosed to the other side prior to the hearing itself so that no one is taken by surprise by the other side's position. In addition, a schedule of assets should be placed before the court. This is simply a document that lists all the assets, owned either individually or jointly, that the court will have to consider.

The petitioner should 'open' the case by simply telling the court the history of the marriage, including relevant dates such as those of the marriage itself, house purchase and the birth of relevant children. She should then refer the district judge to the affidavits relied upon and to the court bundle.

After the petitioner has told the court about her financial state she will be cross-examined by the respondent. The district judge might also have questions to ask her. She can then call any witnesses she chooses to confirm what she has said about her financial situation. If, for instance, the petitioner now has a job which pays less than her previous one, and the respondent does not believe her, a colleague might be produced to confirm her salary.

Any evidence of this sort should first have been put in affidavit form and then served on the other side, although courts do sometimes allow surprise witnesses at the last moment. In this situation the giving of evidence is at the district judge's discretion.

Equal Division of Assets

Short, childless marriages can cause complications: sometimes a straightforward equal division of assets is agreed to, while at other times one party just wishes to repay however much money the other has put into the home. The needs aspect here will be balanced against the entitlement. Where an equal division is in dispute the court might have to hear evidence of what one party has actually contributed, or of the length of time the parties cohabited if they did so before getting married.

What the Court Considers in Questions of Maintenance

Children

The Child Support Agency now deals with child maintenance. If you telephone the Agency's local office they will
send you a form requesting information on your financial status and the suspected financial status of the other party from
whom you are seeking payment.

It is unlikely that a court will waiver a petitioner's claim for
maintenance from her husband for herself while she has
children under the age of eighteen or still in full-time education. Even if she is working successfully, a court will usually
expect the petitioner to have one penny per annum maintenance for herself, to be extinguished at the time that the
children leave home. This is so that the petitioner retains a
foot in the door to come against the respondent should she
subseqently lose her job.

Working Wives

The question of whether the ex-wife should earn her living is
quite a subjective one, and each case tends to be treated on its
own merits. If, for instance, she has not previously had a job
and is still looking after young children, the court is unlikely
to put her in the position where she has to go out to work; it
will, however, probably expect her to do so when all the
children have reached school age. Likewise, if a woman does
not have small children but is over a certain age (say forty)
and has never worked, the court will not necessarily expect
her to start doing so now.

But in the case of a reasonably young woman unencum-
bered by pre-school-age children, her protestations that she
has no experience of the workplace will probably not wash.
The least a court will expect her to do is find a clerical job
where minimal qualifications are required, or to work on the
counter in a store. The courts do, however, take the state of
the job market and the economy into account.

Other Circumstances to Be Taken into Account

The courts also consider matters such as:

- likely inheritance from an elderly relative with an unmortgaged home
- remarriage and any associated financial gain
- the age of the divorced couple
- the duration of the marriage
- pensions (see Chapter 10)

If one party has substantially dissipated the family's assets without due reason – through gambling, say, or expensive shopping habits – the court will take this behaviour into account when a final order is made.

Sale and Transfer of Property

The court has the power to order the valuation and sale of any property in which either husband or wife has a beneficial interest, and to select a solicitor to conduct the sale. The order for sale can be made at the same time as orders for secured periodical payments, lump sums or property adjustment; however, it cannot come into effect until decree absolute has been pronounced. The court can dictate how the proceeds of the sale should be divided. If one side fails to sell the home, the court can order other assets, say shares, to be sold to compensate the waiting partner if she makes the appropriate application.

If someone else has a share in the former family home (see Chapter 8) they will have the right to be heard, but the court can still order a sale irrespective of the interest of someone who is not a former husband or wife.

The former home can be settled upon one party to the divorce or both. If one partner wishes to buy the other out, the court can order the sale to be postponed to allow the buyer to raise the necessary money. The sale can also be postponed in other circumstances, for example:

- until the youngest child is either eighteen or has ceased full-time education, whichever is later, or
- until one party decides to cohabit with someone else, or

- until one party marries again, or
- until one party dies

The court will not transfer the former family home to the wife if she cannot afford the mortgage payments, unless the local DSS office has indicated (which it rarely does in advance) that it will make these payments on her behalf.

Property adjustment orders can be made for any children of the family – property can be transferred to the child or even to another person on the child's behalf. Usually these orders relate to the former family home, but they can also relate to property within that home.

Calderbank Letters

Both petitioner and respondent have the right to make what is called a Calderbank offer – an offer in the form of a letter to the other side that cannot be disclosed to the court in the course of a trial. If, for example, the respondent rejects the petitioner's offer and ends up with less on the decision of the court, the Calderbank letter can be produced to show what the petitioner was offering. The question of the respondent paying the petitioner's costs from the date of the Calderbank letter to the date of the hearing can then be considered by the district judge.

Calderbank letters are a complex business, and it is probably not advisable to consider using them without advice from a solicitor.

At a final hearing the court will expect both parties to submit open letters in addition to the secret Calderbank letters, setting out their open position – that is, exactly what they want and why.

Consent Orders

Even at the door of the court, there is nothing to stop the two parties negotiating an agreement by consent. If the respondent, for example, now agrees to an offer that the petitioner originally sought but that was initially rejected, this is obviously a good reason to agree.

But the consent order must still be passed by the court because the district judge, having read all the associated affidavits, has a duty to ensure fairness. This is especially so where, for example, a clean break (see below) is being made, as a result of which the petitioner will no longer be seeking periodical payments from the respondent.

The district judge will want to be satisfied that the petitioner has sufficient income to support herself, or that, if she is in a slightly precarious financial position but wants nothing from the respondent, then at least she fully understands what she is doing. Also, wherever there are children the court will ensure that the financial arrangement in any consent order properly reflects their needs, irrespective of any clean break between their parents.

The Clean Break

A clean break allows the two parties to become totally independent of each other. A psychological factor is involved: divorcing couples often feel a need to split completely from each other, and financial dependence can be an unhappy reminder. Most clean breaks take place where there is sufficient money to go round – typically, when there will be enough capital from the sale of the family home to enable both partners to rehouse themselves.

Even where there are insufficient funds at this stage to rehouse both partners, if each is holding down a good job then a clean break can often still be achieved. This is because mortgages can be raised in the knowledge that enough income will be available to make the repayments.

But a clean break is not always sought by the parties to the divorce – sometimes courts impose it because they feel that it is the best thing for the couple in question. Conversely, where a clean break is requested but one party would be financially vulnerable, the court might not allow it.

It is, however, unlikely that a court will impose a clean break where one is resisted, even if on the facts it would be an appropriate order to make. Sometimes, to protect a wife a court might still order the husband to pay maintenance, but only at the notional rate of one penny per annum. Technically this is not a clean break, because it still enables the wife to come back to court if necessary and seek maintenance from the husband.

The only orders allowable in a true clean break situation concern lump sums or property adjustment – where the respondent transfers an amount of money or his share of the former family home. The questions of maintenance and any other applications, including applications under the Inheritance Act 1975 for money from the estate of the other party if they were to die, are dismissed.

If there are children still entitled to financial support (see below), this factor will not preclude a clean break between the parents and will not preclude the respondent, say, from paying maintenance for the children.

Financially, a clean break can mean:

- the wife keeps the house but receives no maintenance
- the husband does not get the house but pays the wife no maintenance
- the husband and wife share the proceeds of the sale of the house, and neither pays the other maintenance

Changing Circumstances

Where a clean break is not ordered, the parties must accept that changing financial circumstances in subsequent years may demand a rethink. If, for instance, the former husband loses his job and is therefore unable to make the maintenance payments originally ordered, the two parties will either have to agree reduced payments or return to court to obtain a legal ruling. In such circumstances it is best for both former spouses to try to be realistic. Reduced maintenance payments may not be very attractive, but going to court to try to force a man to pay what he cannot afford costs money too.

Payments for Children: Lump Sum

An application can be made to the court for a lump sum to be awarded to a parent in order to buy, for example, a bed, a refrigerator or some carpet for a child of the family to make use of. The application is dealt with through the courts and not through the Child Support Agency, and can be made at any stage of the divorce proceedings, or after the divorce, under the Children Act 1989. The court will consider:

- needs
- income
- earning capacity
- property and other financial resources
- resources
- standard of living
- any physical or mental disability
- the manner in which the children were previously educated or trained, and the manner in which the parents expect them to be educated or trained

How to Apply for Maintenance for a Child

The Child Support Act 1991 has removed the ability of one party to apply to the court for maintenance for a child, and therefore also the ability of the court to award maintenance for a child.

Now the party will first contact their local Child Support Agency office and then fill in the form which will be sent to them. If the parent with care is working, he or she can still go back to court for the time being if there is an existing maintenance order.

The Child Support Agency came into being particularly to chase absent parents where the parent with care of the children was on a state benefit. The scheme also attracts applications from parents with care of the children who are working but who nevertheless need or cannot get maintenance from the absent parent, and who do not have an existing court order. The absent parent might send money to the parent with care who is working, for instance, but it might not be enough to support the children. Where there is a disagreement of this kind, the Child Support Agency will make the calculation of what is needed.

If the parent with care is frightened to divulge information on the absent parent's whereabouts – perhaps because a child was born without the absent parent's knowledge or in the course of an affair, or the absent parent has a record of abuse or violence – the parent with care can state to the Agency that divulging such information will cause distress. It will then be up to the Agency to decide whether or not to press for the information and seek maintenance from the absent parent. The Agency is now on the brink of ordering payments in the region of 20% of the take-home pay of the absent parent after necessary deductions. This would make what has been a very complex system much more simple.

Considering the Calculation

When making the calculation the following are taken into account:

- the day-to-day costs of maintaining a child
- the incomes of both the parent who has care and the absent parent, taking into consideration tax, national insurance, rental and mortgage expenses, and other children for whom either parent cares or is financially responsible

The Partners of Parents

The partners of either parent will not be expected to pay towards the maintenance of any children who are not theirs.

The Absent Parent

This parent is entitled to contact the Child Support Agency and volunteer financial information before the Agency makes contact.

When the parent with care fills in the form regarding the absent parent, the Agency will try to locate the latter through official Inland Revenue or national insurance records (assuming the address is not already known). Once the address is known, it will only be divulged with the absent parent's agreement. If, once located, the absent parent refuses to cooperate, he will be at risk of receiving a higher maintenance calculation from the Agency.

If the absent parent is receiving Income Support, is over

eighteen, is fit for work, and has no dependent children living at home, there could be a required calculation of £2.20 a week.

Cost of the Agency

The cost of all this to the Agency is about £44 per annum for assessment and review, and £34 per annum for collection. The parties will be expected to pay unless:

- they or their partner receive Income Support, Working Families Credit or Disability Working Allowance
- they are under sixteen, or under nineteen and in full-time education up to A-level or the equivalent
- their income falls below certain limits

Since April 1995 the maintenance formula has been as follows, though it is likely to change to a broad figure of 20 per cent:

1. An absent parent will not be assessed to pay more than 30 per cent of normal net income in current child maintenance or more than 33 per cent in current maintenance.
2. A broad-brush adjustment will be a part of the maintenance formula which will take into account previous 'clean break', final, property or capital settlements.
3. An allowance will be granted for high travel-to-work costs.
4. Housing costs for a new partner or step-parent will be granted.

Since April 1997, parents with care on Income Support or a Jobseeker's Allowance have been able to build up a 'maintenance credit', up to a maximum amount of £1,000, which is paid back to them from the Treasury when they start working again for at least sixteen hours per week.

7

Children: Contact and Residency

Young people are children in the eyes of the law until they reach the age of eighteen, and the differences in law between children born within marriage and those born outside have now been mostly eliminated. When a court evaluates a child's future after the parents have divorced, the main consideration will be the child's welfare.

Conflict over Children at the Start of the Divorce

If the petitioner and respondent cannot agree about the statement of arrangements for children when the petition is originally filed, a hearing will have to be held to decide the matter. There will first be a directions hearing, at which a district judge will hear from both parties. Where the conflict between the parents is obvious, some (but not all) courts offer the service of a court welfare officer, who will speak to them together and/or separately and report her findings to the court. If the court does not have a welfare officer available that day, it will consider the conflict between the parents over the arrangements for the children and then order a welfare report to be produced by a welfare officer. A trial date will be set, perhaps three months from the date of the directions hearing.

Orders Concerning Children

Under section 8 of the Children Act 1989, at the start of divorce proceedings various orders regarding children can be sought from the court by a parent. (There is, however, a presumption that where there is no conflict between the parents concerning their children there should be no formal order of the court. In this situation responsibility for the children remains with both parents after divorce.)

Residence Orders

Formerly known as custody orders, these relate to where the child is going to live. Technically, neither parent is preferred over the other, but if a father has left the former family home and the mother and children remain, it is unlikely that a court will award him residency. Conversely, if it is the mother who has walked out on the family, the father stands an excellent chance of gaining residency. The interest of the child is, as ever, paramount, and the parent remaining in the family home is the one most likely to be able to offer the security of continuity.

Contact Orders

Formerly known as access orders, these state when the parent who has not been awarded residency is going to have contact with the child. Importance is attached by the courts to the children remaining in touch with the parent, and not the other way round, as parents often suppose.

Difficult parents may try to deny contact to their former spouse as a form of revenge. This kind of behaviour is actively discouraged by the courts, who will be thoroughly displeased with the offender. If problems of this sort arise, contact centres run by local authorities can be a useful alternative. Here, children can meet their other parent under the eye of social workers.

But parents can get their wishes in subtler, more devious ways: one parent may prejudice the child against the other so much that contact simply will not work. Because the child's interests are paramount, if the child just does not want to go and see the other parent the court will not force the issue. One of the most galling situations for the 'victim parent' arises if he or she cannot see their child but has to go on paying maintenance.

Contact is about continuity, irrespective of marital break-

down, for the sake of the child. The offending parent should
realise that continuity and familiarity, with the child still see-
ing the parent who has left home, are most likely to help the
child accept the breakdown of the parents' marriage.

Disputes over Residence and Contact

In both residency and contact disputes the courts may well
seek the guidance of a court welfare officer (see above), who
interviews each parent in their separate home and offers the
court independent advice. Courts' views are often heavily
influenced by these reports, though judges can be impressed
by a particular parent in a way that is not highlighted in the
welfare report or even missed altogether.

How to Apply for Residence/Contact Orders

Either parent can file a residency application. You fill in the
standard court form (see p.098 and attach a statement setting
out why you believe you are the better parent and why the
child should come and live with you or continue to do so.
You should include any details that will assist the court to
come to a decision, though the court will not be interested in
what one parent has done to the other unless:

- it has clearly had an adverse effect on the child, or
- it demonstrates that the other parent is incapable of being a
  carer

Copies of this form should be sent both to the court and to the
other parent. Similar application forms exist regarding contact. Once filled in, they should be dealt with in the same way.

If you receive a contact or residency application you can
then draft a statement in reply. It should:

- set out whatever objections you might have
- suggest who you believe the child should be with, and
- suggest what contact you believe should take place

If one parent is denying the other one contact with their child,
it is highly likely that a court welfare officer will be asked to
report on:

- the degree of hate, and the reasons for it (known by the courts as the element of acrimony)
- allegations by one parent about the other
- and, most importantly, the interest of the child

Copies of her report will be sent to the court and to both parents.

Once the court office has received the standard forms, you will be given a date for the hearing.

The Hearing

Because the court welfare officer is a busy person, she is likely to give evidence to the judge first, so that she can then be released. If one parent disagrees with what the welfare officer has said they should cross-examine, suggest a differing view and wait for her reply. If one parent believes that something vital has been overlooked or that the court welfare officer has been biased, all these thoughts should be put to her in the form of legally phrased questions, like this:

- I suggest to you that you didn't listen to what I said when you came to interview me
- I suggest to you that you are biased

Remember that this stage is for questioning a witness, not for making statements of your own. During the course of the trial both parents will have an opportunity to say whatever they want.

Witnesses

If a parent has witnesses, such as grandparents, aunts or friends of the family, who can say that that parent is capable, they can accompany him or her to court to give evidence. However, court rules insist that any statement these witnesses wish to make verbally in court should first be made in writing and served on the other side at least fourteen days before the hearing. The statement should simply give the name and address of the witness, then go on to state what it is they wish to say. It need not be a sworn affidavit if it relates to children.

8

Other Parties Involved in the Divorce

It is not only the two people immediately involved in a divorce who have an interest in the court's decision. An obvious example of an interested party is a bank or building society which has provided mortgage facilities on a family home which is now to be sold or have its ownership transferred. In such circumstances, interested parties are invited to 'intervene' – in other words, to attend the hearing and put their own points across. Such 'intervenors' might belong to any of the groups described below.

Mortgagees

The consent of the mortgagee (building society, bank or other lender for the purpose of house purchase) is required before the family home can be transferred from one party to another, even if the home has been bought in their joint names. Consent will not usually be withheld unless the lender is worried that the new owner will not be able to afford the repayments. If the intended recipient of the home has a low income, he or she should try to secure a guarantor such as the Department of Social Security to satisfy both the lender and, in due course, the court.

Often the DSS will meet the mortgage repayments for the purchase of a home (though not payments on a mortgage taken out to make improvements), but they will not put this in writing before a court hearing. If they did, anyone trying to obtain a transfer of the family home but lacking adequate funds would be placed in a stronger position.

Additional Owners of the Former Family Home

These are known in legal language as 'beneficial owners besides'. If, for instance, a parent of one half of the divorcing couple had provided the deposit for the purchase of the home and now seeks its return, they should 'intervene' so that the court can decide upon their interest.

Creditors

When the marriage breaks down one of the partners might be bankrupt. If so, his trustee in bankruptcy (the person who represents his creditors – those to whom he owes money), might stake a claim on his only asset – the family home – to settle a debt. Alternatively, one of the creditors might have obtained judgement against him (a court order that he must meet a debt) and might, again, be seeking to satisfy the judgement by making a claim on his only asset.

A creditor or trustee can seek a sale of the home under the Trusts for Land and Appointment of Trustees Act 1996. The court will then consider the competing claims of the various parties. If the trustee in bankruptcy makes such an application under the Insolvency Act 1986, the court must make an order it thinks is just and reasonable, taking into consideration:

- the interests of the creditors
- the conduct of the former spouse insofar as it might have contributed to the bankruptcy
- the income, if any, of the former spouse
- the needs of the children
- the entire circumstances of the case

If the application is made not less than one year after the bankruptcy, the court should allow the creditor's interest to take precedence unless there are exceptional circumstances. These might include the hardship that would be suffered by the wife if she had no home for herself and her children. In this situation the court might place what is called a charge on the property. This would mean that the creditor would be repaid out of the proceeds of the eventual sale of the home, with interest. If there are young children in need of a roof over their heads, the court might go on to state that the creditor cannot enforce the order until the youngest child has reached the age of eighteen or has ceased full-time education, whichever comes later.

Rented Properties

The law concerning landlord and tenant is extremely complex, and problems encountered here at any stage of your divorce would best be referred to a solicitor who specialises in this area. Briefly, this is the situation.

A contractual tenancy in a rented home can be transferred from a tenant to a non-tenant, as long as the non-tenant is a party to the divorce proceedings. If the contractual tenancy is also a protected one under the Rent Act 1977 it can be transferred on or after divorce. The other spouse then receives the tenancy without due assignment.

Secure tenancies can be assigned under the Housing Act 1985. However, if the lease contained a clause preventing assignment the court is unlikely to permit the transfer.

The landlord, be it a local authority or a private person, must be advised of the probable transfer and his wishes must be known at the time of the court hearing; a letter will be enough. If the landlord withholds consent to a transfer with good reason, the court is unlikely to go against his wishes.

Under the Rent Act 1977 a statutory tenancy exists whereby, when a protected fixed term or periodic tenancy comes to its end, the tenant staying on can do so on the same terms as his former contractual tenancy. As the tenancy is deemed to be by personal occupation and not a right in property, a transfer can only be sought under section 53, Schedule 7 of the Family Law Act 1996. The tenancy must still exist at the time of the application. A sole tenant's wife will not lose her right of occupation if she remains in the former home after the husband has left, but will do so when decree absolute is pronounced.

Assured tenancies (those not subject to the Rent Act 1977)

can be transferred on divorce under section S24 of the Matrimonial Causes Act 1973 as amended by the Family Law Act 1996 and under section 7 Schedule I of the Matrimonial Homes Act 1983. Once more, the wife of an assured tenant will still have rights of occupation if her husband leaves, but these rights disappear at the stage of decree absolute.

9

Divorce and the Tax Man

Income Tax

A married man living with his wife for even part of the year is entitled to the married couple's allowance for that tax year. Once divorced, however, a husband and wife are treated as single individuals for income tax purposes.

Children

After divorce, the parent who is the main carer of a child, even where there is a joint residency order, is entitled to single parent assessment. The child in question must be:

- under sixteen at the beginning of the assessment period, or
- in full-time education, or
- eighteen and maintained by that parent for all or part of the relevant tax year

The recipient of maintenance payments has to pay tax on them.

Tax Relief on Mortgages

Paying mortgage instalments on a property entitles the home owner to tax relief, which is usually done through the MIRAS (mortgage interest relief at source) scheme. All this means is that the amount payable is reduced in the first place, so that the home owner does not have to claim tax relief later.

A court cannot force one ex-spouse to pay the other's mortgage, even where it has been laid down that this is what should happen. However, if the court believes the payer can afford the other side's mortgage but is not paying it, it will simply increase the maintenance payment.

As the payer is paying the recipient and not the lender (for eg. a bank) directly, the payer is not entitled to MIRAS. But since the recipient will be using this money to make direct payments on a mortgage in her name, she can seek MIRAS on her own taxable income.

Sometimes the court awards each member of the divorcing couple a percentage of the family home. If, say, the husband wishes to buy out the wife's percentage and raises a loan to do so, he is eligible for tax relief on the interest.

Capital Gains Tax

CGT is payable when you dispose of assets and make a profit, though the first few thousand pounds' worth of profit are always exempt. However, no CGT is charged when husbands and wives dispose of assets between each other.

Homes are treated slightly differently from other assets. No CGT is payable on any profit made when you sell your sole or main residence. Someone who owns more than one property can decide which should be regarded as his main residence for tax purposes. The property selected should have been occupied by him throughout the time of his ownership.

Ex-spouses are considered to be separate individuals for CGT purposes, but again the former family home is an exception. If the home is transferred from one partner to the other after divorce, no capital gains tax is payable as long as the transfer forms part of a court order relating to long-term maintenance (ancillary relief).

When judicially separated or divorced husbands and wives transfer the former family home from one to the other, the spouse who is making the transfer is said for CGT purposes to have remained in occupation until the day of transfer. This ensures that the whole gain (assuming there is one) remains exempt.

The spouse receiving the transfer must have remained in occupation of the property as her main residence. Before the transfer, the other spouse should have chosen any other home as his main residence.

In general, to help divorcing husbands and wives avoid CGT on the former family home there is a two-year moratorium during which gains are exempt. For instance, if the court orders the sale of the home, and the husband, say, pays the wife a lump sum out of the proceeds, he will not be liable for CGT provided the sale takes place within two years of his leaving the home and provided that the wife is still occupying the home.

Again, where the home was bought in joint names, the person who is not the occupier will gain exemption on her share of the proceeds as long as the property is sold within two years of her leaving the home. Whichever former partner is still occupying the home at the time of sale is automatically exempt from CGT.

Where a home is transferred into joint names and its sale is deferred beyond the two-year period described above, the partner who does not remain in occupation may find himself liable to CGT on his share of the proceeds. Similarly, where the wife, for instance, now has the home in her sole name but the court has awarded the husband a certain percentage of the proceeds of its eventual sale, he may have to pay CGT.

CGT can be complex, so it is best to consult an accountant if you have any doubts or worries.

Inheritance Tax

This is a tax that has to be paid when you inherit property on someone's death. Transfers between husband and wife are not liable for inheritance tax, although this exemption is lost when you get divorced. There are, however, certain exceptions. These include the payment of maintenance from one party to the other or to a child of either of them.

Transfers of money are also not liable to inheritance tax since they are known in legal terms as transactions 'at arm's length which are not intended to confer any gratuitous benefit'. The Inland Revenue allows such transactions to be exempt.

The position regarding jointly owned homes can be complicated, and to avoid paying inheritance tax unnecessarily it is worthwhile consulting a solicitor or accountant.

10
Pensions

Within divorce proceedings a husband often has a pension policy whereas his wife does not. Upon divorce the wife almost always loses her claim to the husband's pension policy. If there is enough money from the divorce melting pot she can be compensated by getting extra sums of money from the other assets. If there is no money for compensation there can be some consideration of the wife being apportioned part of her husband's pension.

The two considerations of any judge regarding a pension have been:

Set off

Which permits the division of the matrimonial assets to compensate the wife for any loss of the pension rights of the husband that she would have had had she remained married to him.

Earmarking

Which permits the judge to direct that a part of a pension lump sum that would come into being upon retirement should be paid to the wife for compensation.

Valuation

Before the wife decides exactly which option she should take – set off or earmarking – she will have to find out the value of the pension of the husband.

How to Value

The most sensible way of a wife valuing the pension of a husband is to find out what is called The Cash Equivalent Transfer Value of the pension policy (CETV).

Once the value is known the court can consider making an order that a lump sum be paid from the pension policy upon its maturation – namely, when the husband retires. Many wives may prefer to take advantage of the set off, which permits the wife to take advantage of a compensatory sum of money at the time of the financial proceedings, have the cash and invest it, rather than wait for a number of years and by reason of the waiting still have an element of dependency upon the husband she would prefer to be rid of both emotionally and financially.

A New Law

Petitions for divorce dated after 1 December 2000 permit the court to split the proceedings of the pension fund. This is thought to be a fairer distribution of what is often a major asset of the marriage. A letter must be written to the pension fund seeking the CETV of the pension, their views on a proposed splitting and what they might themselves suggest. Giving a pension fund advance notice of any such application is helpful, as their views can then be ascertained prior to any hearing.

11

Failure to Pay Maintenance

What to Do if You Don't Get Your Maintenance Payment

Where a maintenance order is not complied with – in other words, the husband or father refuses to pay up – various enforcement procedures are available. However, no court will order him to pay maintenance if events that have occurred since the original order was made mean that he no longer has any assets or available income.

To help you deal with non-payment, should it arise, register the order in the magistrates' court (unless it was made in the family proceedings court). Take a copy of the original order to the court counter; the court now becomes the recipient of the payments in the first instance and will hand each one on to the payee.

If you make a complaint that the payments are in arrears, the court will have a hearing to investigate the means of the father or husband who has failed to pay. Often courts suggest payment by instalments to deal with the arrears. However, if arrears have mounted up the court might simply wipe the slate clean (called remitting the arrears) rather than have them continue as a millstone around the father's neck. Obviously, it is best to make your complaint before this situation is reached.

Various other methods of obtaining money are described below.

Attachment of Earnings

An order for what is known as attachment of earnings can be sought in both the magistrates' court and the divorce court. It means that the employer of the man owing the maintenance will deduct this money at source, before he receives his wages or salary. A cheque is immediately sent to the court and then handed over to the mother or wife.

The exact sum sought each month/week must be stated, as well as the sum below which his earnings cannot reasonably fall. It would not make sense for a working father to be living below the poverty line simply to keep up the attachment of earnings order.

The working father or husband has a duty to inform the court if he changes his job.

Judgement Summons

An application for a judgement summons can be brought in the county court. As in the magistrates' court, there will be a hearing on the father/husband's means before an order, probably again by instalments, is made.

Seizure of Assets

An application can be brought in the county court for what is known legally as a writ of fieri facias. This means that the father/husband's goods can be seized and sold to pay off the debt.

Payment from a Third Party

If a third party owes money to the father or husband, an application can be brought in the county court requiring that person to pay the money directly to the mother. This is known as a garnishee order.

Charging Order

Debts can be 'charged' upon the assets of the father/husband, especially any home or land in his name. The mother's interest can be registered at the local Land Registry office to prevent the property being sold without her consent. If and when it is sold, any debt owing to her will come from the proceeds.

Where to Go for Help

Here is a selection of useful organisations; some of them deal with obvious and direct problems, while others provide more general services.

Asian Family Counselling Service 01274 720486
Association of Separated and Divorced Catholics 020 7371 8253
British Association of Counsellors 01788 778328/9
Capital Radio 020 7388 7575
Catholic Marriage Advisory Service 020 7727 0141
Catholic Marriage Guidance Council 020 8371 1341
Child Poverty Action Group 020 7253 3406
Chiswick Family Rescue 020 7995 4430
Citizens' Advice Bureaux (see your local telephone directory)
Family Mediators Association 0117 9500140
Families Need Fathers 020 8886 0970
Gingerbread 020 7240 0953 (and see your local telephone directory). Support and advice for one-parent families
Jewish Marriage Guidance Council 020 8203 6311
Jewish Mediation Service 020 7636 9380
Joint Council for the Welfare of Immigrants 020 7251 8706
Mediation in Divorce 020 8891 6860
National Council for Voluntary Organisations 020 7713 6161
National Association of Family Mediation and Conciliation Services, or Family Mediation for short (formerly the National Family Conciliation Council) 01793 514055. The umbrella organisation for family conciliation services
National Council for the Divorced and Separated Trust 0114 2726331
National Federation of Solo Clubs 0121 2362879
National Foster Care Association 020 7828 6266
National Stepfamily Association 01223 460313

Nexus 020 8359 7656

One Parent Families 020 8267 1361

RELATE (formerly Marriage Guidance Council) 01788 573241

Samaritans 01753 32713 (see also your local telephone directory)

Shelter 020 7254 0202. Round-the-clock help with all kinds of housing problems

Solicitors Family Law Association 01689 850227

Westminster Pastoral Foundation 020 7937 6956

Women's Aid Federation 020 7251 6537. Help for women who are suffering domestic violence

Women's Aid National Office 0117 9428368

Lawyers, Costs and Legal Aid

This is a handbook designed to help you conduct your own divorce. But having read it, you may decide that you would rather someone else did the work. In any case, as pointed out in the preceding chapters, certain aspects of divorce (in particular the financial settlement) are quite complex and you might actually be doing yourself a service if at this stage you consulted a solicitor. But what might it all cost?

Costs

Legal costs spiral upwards with ease. It is easy for the petitioner to lose track of them, since no payment may necessarily be requested during the course of the divorce proceedings.

If a petitioner telephones a solicitor, for instance, that call will be logged and the solicitor's time charged for. VAT is chargeable on top. Clearly it makes sense to ask about rates before committing yourself.

Never forget, either, that work is done, and has to be paid for, that does not necessarily involve you directly – interviewing witnesses, for instance, and attendance at court. If a petitioner has a conference with counsel (the barrister instructed by the solicitor to handle the case), that too will be charged for. If the couple's bank statements or other financial documents are complicated, it is in the petitioner's own interest to peruse them in detail because if counsel has to do it, it will take time and cost money. Remember: time is of the essence.

Legal Aid

Don't be taken in by what you may have heard or read about

legal aid. It is not necessarily free, and there are strict guide-lines concerning who is and is not entitled to it. There are two stages: what is known as the green form scheme, and full legal aid.

Full Legal Aid

In order to qualify for an extension to legal aid, the applicant must have only a limited amount of income and/or capital. Full cover allows you to have a solicitor and a barrister on your case, though the system is not entirely a free one and drawbacks exist. You should have disposable income of no less than about £44 per week to qualify for legal aid without a contribution. However, a figure over that amount could still allow the applicant a legal aid certificate, but he will have to contribute to the legal aid granted. Consideration for legal aid will depend upon expenses such as rent, mortgage, travel to work, dependants and the like.

If in due course the applicant, on order of the court, obtains the family home or a part of the net proceeds of sale (equity), the cost of legal aid will be clawed back. The Legal Aid Board will fix a charge in its favour on the family home. When the house is sold, it will then claw back whatever is owing to it, plus interest since the time of the order.

If the applicant gets a lump sum as a result of a court order, the legal aid charge will eat it up if it is over a certain amount. The only exception is if it is sufficiently large to be used or put towards the purchase of a home: this intended use must be stated in the court order, and the court is likely to enforce this if there are children to be housed. If this occurs, the charge will be deferred until the home is sold.

If you receive no more than £2,500 you will not pay back legal aid. If you receive more than this you might still get legal aid, but you could be required to contribute to your legal aid certificate by paying back whatever you recover or preserve that is more than £2,500.

See Legal Aid Schedule, p.70.

Solicitors

As mentioned above, different firms of solicitors, like barristers, are likely to charge different rates once the fixed-rate stage is past. Local high street firms are less expensive than their counterparts in major towns and cities. This is because their overheads in terms of rent, council tax and so on are likely to be less.

Most high street firms will take legal aid clients. Big city firms are highly unlikely to offer advice to clients on legal aid.

Legal Aid Schedule

A method of calculating eligibility on income:

1. Calculate your household's gross weekly income (including child benefit).
2. Deduct tax, national insurance and expenses in connection with employment, e.g., travel to work, child minder, weekly rent, mortgage payments, rates and council tax.
3. Multiply this figure by 52, but deduct the following dependants' allowances:

Partner	£1,423
Dependant under 11	£ 858
11 to 15	£1,257
16 to 17	£1,504
18+	£1,976

4. This figure is yearly disposable income; if between £2,498 and £7,403, deduct £2,498 and divide by 36. This resulting figure is the contribution from income that you must pay each month during the period that you are legally aided.

Disposable income:

Limit below which no contribution is required – £2,498 per annum

Limit above which legal aid is unavailable – £7,403 per annum (£8,158 per annum for personal injury claims)

If disposable income is between these limits, you may have to pay a monthly contribution towards the cost of legal aid out of your income.

Disposable capital:

Limit below which no contribution is required – £3,000

Limit above which legal aid may be refused – £6,750 (£8,560 for personal injury claims)

If your disposable capital is between these limits, you may have to pay a contribution towards the cost of legal aid out of your capital.

Anyone in receipt of Income Support is eligible, regardless of capital.

If you are a pensioner, then according to the amount of your annual disposable income, an amount of capital may be disregarded for the purpose of assessing your disposable capital.

Annual disposable income	Amount of capital disregarded
up to £370	£35,000
£371–£670	£30,000
£671–£970	£25,000
£971–£1,270	£20,000
£1,270–£1,570	£15,000
£1,571–£1,870	£10,000
£1,871–£2,498	£5,000

Social Security Benefits (Non-means-tested)

1. *Retirement*

Retirement Pension	99–00	00–01
Claimant	61.15	62.45
Non-contributing spouse/ adult dependant – extra	36.60	37.35

Every pensioner aged over 80 receives an additional £0.25 p.w. or £13.00 p.a.

Either spouse may qualify in their own right, or as a dependant.

Special rules apply for married women, divorced people, widows and widowers.

Contributary and taxable.

2. *Ill Health*

i. **Statutory Sick Pay**

	99–00	00–01
Standard rate	59.95	60.20

Paid by the employer for 168 days (28 six-day weeks) to employees earning not less than £62.00 gross p.w.

Taxable.

ii. **Incapacity Benefit**

		99–00	00–01
Long-term		66.75	67.50
Increase for age	Higher rate	14.05	14.20
	Lower rate	7.05	7.10
Adult dependant – extra		39.95	40.40
Short-term (under pension age)			
Lower rate		50.35	50.90
Higher rate		59.95	60.20
Adult dependant – extra		31.15	31.50

Short-term (over pension age)

Lower & Higher rate	64.75	67.50
Adult dependant – extra	38.40	38.80

Incapacity Benefit has replaced Sickness Benefit and Invalidity Benefit. Short-term Incapacity Benefit is payable at the lower rate for 1-28 weeks (incapacity assessed against own job) and at the higher rate from 29 to 52 weeks. Long-term Incapacity Benefit is payable from 52 weeks. After 28 weeks incapacity is assessed on functional limitation.

Contributory.

Taxable for new claimants for short-term higher rate and long-term benefits only; otherwise non-taxable. The age increases are payable at the higher rate if incapacity begins under 35, and at the lower rate if under 45.

iii. Severe Disablement Allowance	99–00	00–01
Claimant	40.35	40.80
Adult dependant – extra	23.95	24.20
Age-related additions		
Higher	14.05	14.20
Middle	8.90	9.00
Lower	4.45	4.50

Paid if 80% disabled, and unfit for work on functional test. Non-contributory and non-taxable.

iv. Invalid Care Allowance	99–00	00–01
Claimant	39.95	40.41
Adult dependant – extra	23.90	24.15

Paid to claimants who care for someone receiving the higher or middle rates of the Care Component of Disability Living Allowance or Attendance Allowance.

Non-contributory. Claimant's benefit is taxable; extra benefit for adult dependant is non-taxable.

3. *Unemployment – Jobseeker's Allowance (JSA)*

i. Contribution-based JSA		99–00	00–01
Claimant	18–24	40.70	41.35
	25 and over	51.40	52.20

ii. Income-based JSA

		99–00	00–01
Claimant	18–24	40.70	41.35
	25 and over	51.40	52.20
Couple. One or both over 18		80.65	81.95
Dependant children			
	Under 15		25.90
	16–18	30.95	31.75

Premiums: as for Income Support. Contributory JSA is flat rate, without allowances for dependants, and paid for 26 weeks. Income-based JSA is paid upon the expiry of the contributory JSA and is modelled on Income Support with similar rules for income, capital premiums and mortgage interest. Claimants must be available for and actively seeking work and have a current Jobseeker's Agreement.

Entitlement to Income-based JSA is a passport to other benefits, including maximum Housing and Council Tax Benefit.

Taxable. Main rates only given. Not usually available for those under 18.

4. *Maternity*
i. Statutory Maternity Pay

	99–00	00–01
Higher rate (first 6 weeks)	90% of average weekly wage	
Earnings threshold	66.00	67.00
Lower rate (next 12 weeks maximum)	59.55	60.20

Paid by the employer for a maximum of 18 weeks.
Taxable

ii. Maternity Allowance

	99–00	00–01
Lower rate	51.70	52.25
Higher rate	59.95	60.20
Adult dependant – extra	31.15	31.50

Paid for 18 weeks to claimants not entitled to Statutory Maternity Pay.

Contributory and non-taxable.

5. *Widowhood*

Widow's Benefit	99–00	00–01
Widow's Payment (lump sum)	1000.00	1000.00
Widowed Mother's Allowance	66.75	67.50
Widow's Pension (age-related)		
45–54	20.03	20.25
	to	to
	62.08	62.78
55 or over	66.75	67.50

A different scale applies for deaths before 11 April 1988. The lump sum widow's payment is contributory and non-taxable.
Weekly benefits are contributory and taxable.

6. *Additional child payments for specified benefits*

	99–00	00–01
Child – extra	11.35	11.35

Paid in addition to long-term income replacement benefits (Retirement Pension, short-term higher rate and long-term Incapacity Benefit, Severe Disablement Allowance, Invalid Care Allowance, Widowed Mother's Allowance and Widow's Pension) and to short-term lower rate Incapacity Benefit if claimant over pensionable age. A child must be under sixteen, or under nineteen and in full-time secondary education. Reduced if overlapping Child Benefit also in payment.

7. *Disability Living Allowance*

		99–00	00–01
Care Component	Higher	52.95	53.55
	Middle	35.40	35.80
	Lower	14.05	14.20
Mobility Component	Higher	37.00	37.40
	Lower	14.05	14.20

The claimant must qualify before reaching 65.
The range of allowances is related to need: no restriction on use of money.
Non-contributory and non-taxable.

8. *Attendance Allowance*

	99–00	00–01
Higher rate	52.95	53.55
Lower rate	35.40	35.50

Paid for care needs of those over 65: no requirement to spend on care.

Non-contributory and non-taxable.

9. *Child Benefit*

	99–00
Only/elder/eldest child	14.40
Only/elder/eldest child of lone parent	17.10
Each subsequent child	9.60

A child must be under 16, or under 19 and in full-time secondary education.

Non-contributory and non-taxable.

10. *Guardian's Allowance*

	99–00
Claimant	11.35

Reduced if overlapping Child Benefit also in payment.
Non-contributory and non-taxable.

Types of Courts and Their Responsibilities

Courts

Can deal with applications concerning, among other topics:

- parental responsibility
- residence
- contact
- specific issues
- prohibited steps orders
- maintenance and separation orders
- injunctions regarding domestic violence in connection with married/unmarried persons
- payment of lump sums up to £1000 to a spouse/child in family proceedings

Difficult cases regarding children can be sent by the family proceedings court to higher courts.

The majority of appeals on family matters are dealt with by the Family Division of the High Court.

County Court

Can deal with all the matters mentioned above, plus:

- divorce
- nullity cases
- judicial separation
- property issues
- lump sum payments
- costs

Appeals from judges of the county court go to the Court of Appeal. Appeals from district judges go mostly to the county court judge.

High Court (Family Division)

Can deal with any of the matters sent to it by the lower courts.

Court of Appeal

Can deal with cases referred to it by the lower court on a matter of law only.

House of Lords

Can deal with cases referred to it by the lower court on a matter of law only.

Choosing a Court

The family proceedings court is the easiest and cheapest court in which to make applications, but it only has power to award lump sums up to £1,000. Therefore if the financial provision you are seeking includes a family home and savings you must go to the county court. If you have started financial application in the county court and then want to bring a residency application, it is sensible to begin that in the same county court so that everything is tied up in one place.

List of Divorce County Courts

Aberystwyth
Accrington
Aldershot and Farnham
Altrincham
Andover
Barnet
Barnsley
Barnstaple
Barrow-in-Furness
Basingstoke
Bath
Bedford

Birkenhead
Birmingham
Bishop Auckland
Blackburn
Blackpool
Blackwood
Bodmin
Bolton
Boston
Bow (London)
Bradford
Brentford

Bridgend
Bridgwater
Brighton
Bristol
Bromley
Burnley
Burton-on-Trent
Bury
Bury St Edmunds
Caernarfon
Camborne and Redruth
Cambridge
Canterbury
Cardiff
Carlisle
Carmarthen
Chelmsford
Chester
Chesterfield
Chichester
Chippenham
Chorley
Colchester
Consett
Coventry
Crewe
Croydon
Darlington
Derby
Dewsbury
Dolgellau
Doncaster
Dudley
Durham
Eastbourne
Edmonton (London)
Epsom
Exeter
Gateshead
Gloucester
Great Grimsby

Guildford
Halifax
Harlow
Harrogate
Hartlepool
Hastings
Haverfordwest
Hereford
Hitchin
Horsham
Huddersfield
Hull (Kingston-upon-Hull)
Ilford
Ipswich
Keighley
Kendal
King's Lynn
Kingston-upon-Thames
Lancaster
Leeds
Leicester
Leigh
Lincoln
Liverpool
Llanelli
Llangefni
London (Bow, Edmonton,
    Wandsworth, Willesden)
Lowestoft
Luton
Macclesfield
Maidstone
Manchester
Mansfield
Medway (Kent)
Merthyr Tydfil
Milton Keynes
Neath and Port Talbot
Nelson
Newcastle-upon-Tyne
Newport (Gwent)

Newport (Isle of Wight)
Northampton
North Shields
Norwich
Nottingham
Oldham
Oxford
Penrith
Peterborough
Plymouth
Pontefract
Pontypridd
Portsmouth
Preston
Rawtenstall
Reading
Reigate
Rhyl
Rochdale
Romford
Rotherham
Runcorn
St Helens
Salford
Salisbury
Scarborough
Scunthorpe
Sheffield
Shrewsbury
Skipton
Slough
Southampton
Southend
Southport
South Shields
Stafford
Staines

Stockport
Stockton-on-Tees
Stoke-on-Trent
Sunderland
Swansea
Swindon
Tameside
Taunton
Teesside
Telford
Thanet (Kent)
Trowbridge
Truro
Tunbridge Wells
Uxbridge
Wakefield
Walsall
Wandsworth (London)
Warrington
Watford
Welshpool and Newtown
West Bromwich
Weston-super-Mare
Weymouth
Whitehaven
Wigan
Willesden (London)
Winchester
Wolverhampton
Worcester
Workington
Worthing
Wrexham
Yeovil
York

Principal Registry

Court Orders: Appeals and Variations

Appealing Against a Court Order

An order made by a district judge can be appealed against, but only with good reason. It would not be fair to suggest that you could handle an appeal without professional assistance: it makes better sense to instruct a solicitor. However, the appeal process is outlined here so that the various stages will not be totally unfamiliar.

First, an application called a notice of appeal, together with the reasons why the order is being appealed against (the grounds for the appeal) must be served upon the other side and filed at the court.

The appeal is heard before the judge, and simply consists of a rehearing of the case. Any new or recent evidence not presented to the previous court can be placed before the appeal court.

A further level of appeal is possible, to the Court of Appeal. But this can only be made on a point of law – if it is alleged that a judge has not applied a statute properly. Appeals are often sought on the ground that by giving a favourable judgement to the other party a judge has failed to use his discretion properly.

Setting Aside a Court Order

If you want an order of the court to be set aside, you fill in a preliminary application and send it to the court in the usual way. There is no time limit, though the longer you wait the more difficult it may be to obtain permission (leave) to make the application to set the order aside. The power to grant or reject this permission lies with the judge.

There are many reasons why you might seek to set an order aside. Often the two parties in a divorce are not full and frank when disclosing documents: a petitioner wife, for instance, might discover after the court hearing and judgement that the respondent owns far more assets than he previously revealed. Had the court known about these additional assets, it would have made a different order.

Where property is concerned, if a house falls or rises substantially in value, or was wrongly valued through some genuine error, this could change the basis of an order. Say, for instance, a judge believed a house was worth £100,000 and it then sold for £150,000, or vice versa, this would affect a previous court order.

As a rule courts dislike setting aside an order where events following its issue might be said to have changed the basis on which it was originally made. The subsequent occurrence must be very grave, or the courts will simply refuse the application and the order will have to stand.

Varying a Court Order

If you wish to vary an order, you must give notice to the other side by means of an ordinary court form of notice; leave is not required. The respondent should receive his copy of the application within four days of your filing it at the court.

The applicant usually files an affidavit setting out the reasons for bringing the application. If the respondent is willing, an application can be made with the consent of both parties. The court will look again at the original circumstances and at those which are relevant to the application for variation.

Orders that can be varied are:

- periodical payments and secured periodical payment orders
- lump sum instalment order payments
- settlement of property or variation of settlement
- sale of property orders

Orders can also be discharged and suspended, while arrears of maintenance can be remitted – that is, wiped clean. But whilst you can apply for an extension of the time limit for the making of periodical payments, the court can pre-empt this by including in the order a direction that no such application may be made.

It is not possible to vary a periodical payments order by making a property adjustment order or lump sum order. However, a lump sum variation can be made for a child of the family and a maintenance order can be discharged if there is an understanding to make a capital lump sum payment instead. Orders for lump sums can be varied where the sum was to be paid in instalments.

Any variation can be postponed or backdated. Applications to suspend or discharge orders should be made to the court that made the order in the first place.

Where an order has been made for the sale of a house at a future date, either party can seek to have the property sold if the order has not been complied with. It is up to the court to decide whether the application should be granted.

Documents Used in Divorce Proceedings

Court Forms

Court forms are simply documents that have been standardised to make life easier for parties to a divorce regarding whatever applications or defences they may be making. These documents can be picked up at court counters.

The following are examples of the various forms usually required in the course of the divorce process, though they are by no means every document relating to the divorce procedure.

In the main they are self-explanatory. The financial forms simply request the party to answer the individual questions posed as to income and expenditure, savings, mortgages, pensions and so on, so that financial information is collated easily and speedily.

Where the financial situation of the parties is straightforward in that they are employed, taxed PAYE and have savings that are easily located, the standard court form will probably suffice, and there will be no need to swear other affidavits regarding financial means, unless of course there are going to be allegations of misappropriation of assets and the like.

Here are the forms:

1

IN THE LONDON COUNTY COURT   NUMBER:

BETWEEN: RENE MARKS PETITIONER

AND

JACK MARKS RESPONDENT

PETITION OF DIVORCE

1. On the 10th of July 1975 the Petitioner, Rene Marks, was lawfully married to Jack Marks (hereinafter called the Respondent) at St Adolf's Church, in the Parish of Calder in the County of London.

2. The Petitioner and Respondent last lived together at Hilltops, Lampstead, the County of London.

3. The Petitioner is domiciled in England and Wales and is by occupation a Designer and resides at Hilltops, Lampstead, the County of London.

4. There are no children of the family now living except Mark Menelaus who was born on August the 2nd 1978 and is receiving full time education at University College School, London.

5. There are no other proceedings in any court in England or Wales or elsewhere with reference to the marriage, or to any children of the family or between the Petitioner and the Respondent with reference to any property of either or both of them except that on March 2nd 1991 at London County Court the Respondent was ordered to pay maintenance to the Petitioner on behalf of the one child of the family at the rate of £200 per month and residency of the said child was vested in the Petitioner on January 6th 1992.

6. There are no proceedings continuing in any country outside England and Wales which are in respect of the marriage or are capable of affecting its validity or existence.

7. The said marriage has broken down irretrievably.

8. The Respondent has behaved unreasonably and the Petitioner finds it intolerable to live with the Respondent.

10. PARTICULARS

On December 18th 1991 the Respondent returned to the former matrimonial home in a drunken state, he went into the

1

kitchen and grabbed the Petitioner by the throat, pulling her on to the kitchen table and attempted to force her to have intercourse with him. The next day whilst the Petitioner was in the bathroom he entered without invitation and tried to force her to have intercourse on the bathroom's floor without her consent. During this occasion she suffered bruising to her back, her left leg, her right arm and bleeding to her face.

PRAYER

The Petitioner therefore prays:

1. That the said marriage be dissolved.

2. That the residency of Mark Menelaus be vested in the Petitioner.

3. That the Respondent may be ordered to pay the costs of this suit, if defended.

4. That the Petitioner may be granted the following ancillary relief:
    (a) an order for maintenance pending suit
    a periodical payments order
    a secured provision order
    a lump sum order
    (b) a periodical payments order for the child of the family
    a secured provision order for the child of the family
    a lump sum order for the child of the family
    (c) a property adjustment order

Signed Rene Marks

The name and addresses of the persons to be served with this Petition are:

Respondent: Jack Marks, of Black Cottage, Tighgate, in the County of London

The Petitioner's address for service is: C/o Sparks, Candia Way, Lockleigh, the County of London

DATED

ADDRESS all communications to London County Court at

2

IN THE LONDON COUNTY COURT   NUMBER:

BETWEEN: RENE MARKS PETITIONER

AND

JACK MARKS RESPONDENT

The Respondent in answer to the Petition filed in this suit, says as follows;

1. He admits the matters set out in paragraphs one to seven of the Petition.

2. So far as is known to the Respondent no other child now living has been born to the Petitioner during the said marriage.

3. He admits and avers that the said marriage has broken down irretrievably but denies that such breakdown has been caused by his behaviour as alleged or at all.

4. As to paragraph eight of the Petition he denies that he has behaved in such a way that the Petitioner cannot reasonably be expected to live with him. Save as is hereinafter expressly admitted he denies each and every allegation contained in the Particulars stated at paragraph ten.

(a) He denies that he was drunk when he returned to the former matrimonial home on December 18th 1991 and denies that he grabbed the Petitioner by her throat.

(b) He admits that he pulled her on to the kitchen table and attempted to force her to have intercourse with him.

(c) He denies that he entered the bathroom when the Petitioner was within without her due invitation.

(d) He avers that the Petitioner sought to have intercourse upon the floor of the very bathroom with him.

(e) He denies that she suffered any injury whatsoever.

SIGNED

The names and addresses of the persons to be served with this ANSWER are

(insert any name and address of Solicitors of the Petitioner or the address of the Petitioner herself if unrepresented)

The Respondent's address for service is:

Black Cottage, Tighgate, London

3

IN THE LONDON COUNTY COURT   NUMBER:

BETWEEN: RENE MARKS PETITIONER

AND

JACK MARKS RESPONDENT

The Petitioner in REPLY to the Answer filed in this suit, says that:

1. Save in so far as the same consists of admissions she denies each and every allegation contained in the said ANSWER and joins issue with the Respondent thereon.

2. She avers that the Respondent entered the bathroom without her due invitation and that he sought to have intercourse with her upon the bathroom floor.

3. She avers that she suffered injury.

The Petitioner therefore prays:

(1) As before

TO: Jack Marks, Black Cottage, Tighgate, London

4

FAMILY PROCEEDINGS RULES

*Complete and/or delete as appropriate.

If proceeding in a District Registry, delete both headings and insert "In the High Court of Justice, Family Division District Registry".

IN THE _____ **COUNTY COURT***

PRINCIPAL REGISTRY*

No. of Matter

Between..Petitioner

and ....Respondent

(1) Name, address and description

I,(1)

of

make oath and say: -

1. That a copy of the Petition bearing date the   day of

     19   filed in these proceedings together with a Notice of

Proceedings and an Acknowledgement of Service

.

was duly served by me on

.

the   in this case at

.

on the   day of   19   by delivering to the said

.

personally a   copy thereof.

(2) In the case of the respondent, insert here the means of knowledge of the identity of the person served, e.g. a photograph or description.

2. (2) And I further make oath and say

SWORN at

this   day of   19

Before me

A Commissioner for Oaths/Solicitor

Notice of Application for Decree Nisi to be made Absolute.
(Form M8, Appendix 1, F.P.R. 1991)

FAMILY PROCEEDINGS RULES

IN THE————————— **COUNTY COURT***

PRINCIPAL REGISTRY*

Rule 2.49(1)

*Complete
and/or delete as
appropriate.
If proceeding in a
District Registry,
delete both head-
ings and insert "in
the High Court of
Justice, Family
Division, District
Registry".

No. of Matter

Between..Petitioner

and ....Respondent

TAKE NOTICE that the Petitioner

applies for the decree nisi pronounced in his (her) favour on the

day of   19   , to be made absolute.

Dated this   day of   19

Signed ....
Solicitors for Petitioner

of ....

....

Address all communications for the Court to: The Chief Clerk, County Court*...

....

(or to the Principal Registry, Somerset House, Strand, London WC2R 1LP) quoting the number in the top right-hand corner of this form.
The Court Office is open from 10 a.m. till 4 p.m. (4.30 p.m. at the Principal Registry) on Mondays to Fridays only.

5

NOTICE
of Application for Decree Nisi
to be made Absolute

OYEZ The Solicitors' Law Stationery Society Ltd.   1991 Edition
Oyez House, 7 Spa Road, London SE16 3QQ   8.91 F20676
5046842

Divorce 100

6

Notice of [Intention to Proceed with] an Application for Ancillary Relief

In the	
*[County Court] *[Principal Registry of the Family Division]	
Case No. *Always quote this*	
Applicant's Solicitor's reference	
Respondent's Solicitor's reference	

(*delete as appropriate)

Postcode

(Name and Address of Respondent(s) / Respondent(s) Solicitors

The marriage of   **and**

Take Notice that

the Applicant intends **to apply** to the Court or **to proceed** with the application in the [petition][answer] for:

- [ ] an order for maintenance pending suit
- [ ] a secured provision order
- [ ] a property adjustment order
- [ ] a periodical payments order
- [ ] a lump sum order

If an application is made for any periodical payments or secured periodical payments for children:

- and there is a written agreement made before 5 April 1993 about maintenance for the benefit of children, **tick this box** [ ]

- and there is a written agreement made on or after 5 April 1993 about maintenance for the benefit of children, **tick this box** [ ]

- but there is no agreement, tick any of the boxes below to show if you are applying for payment:

  - [ ] for a stepchild or stepchildren
  - [ ] in addition to child support maintenance already paid under a Child Support Agency assessment
  - [ ] to meet expenses arising from a child's disability
  - [ ] to meet expenses incurred by a child in being educated or training for work
  - [ ] when either the child **or** the person with care of the child **or** the absent parent of the child is not habitually resident in the United Kingdom
  - [ ] Other (please state)

Signed: Dated:

[XXXXXX][Solicitor for the Applicant]

The Court Office at

open 10 am and 4 pm (4.30pm at the Principal Registry of the Family Division) Monday to Friday. When corresponding with the court, please address forms or letters to the Court Manager and quote the case number. If you do not do so, your correspondence may be returned.

Form A Notice of [Intention to Proceed with] an Application for Ancillary Relief

FORM A/1

7

Statement of information for a consent order.

| FAMILY PROCEEDINGS RULES | IN THE ———————————— | COUNTY COURT PRINCIPAL REGISTRY |

Rule 2.61
(M.1)

No. of Matter

*Complete and/or delete as appropriate.

Between .... Petitioner

and .... Respondent

Duration of marriage:	Ages of Parties
	Age of Petitioner: Age of Respondent:
	Age(s) of any minor or dependent child(ren) (i.e. under the age(s) of 18):

Note	Summary of means
If the application is only for an order for interim periodical payments or variation of an order for periodical payments then only the information required under 'net income' need be given.	Give as the date of the statement the approximate amount or value of capital resources and net income of Petitioner and Respondent and, where relevant, of minor child(ren) of the family. State also the net equity in any property concerned and the effect of its proposed distribution.

	Capital resources (less any unpaid mortgage or charge)	Net income
Petitioner		
Respondent		
Child(ren)		

[P.T.

7

here the parties are to live.

ve details of what arrangements are intended for the accommodation of each of the parties and any minor child(ren) the family.

arital plans.

ase tick a box.

Petitioner	Respondent	
☐	☐	has no present intention to marry or co-habit
☐	☐	has remarried
☐	☐	intends to marry
☐	☐	intends to co-habit with another person

Note

o be answered by
e applicant where
e terms of the
rder provide for a
ansfer of property.

Notice to mortgagee.

Has any and every mortgagee of the property been served with notice of the application?

Yes ☐   No ☐

Has any objection to such a transfer been made by any mortgagee within 14 days from the date of service?

Yes ☐   No ☐

her information.   Give details of any other especially significant matters.

gnatures

gned) ....Date...(Solicitor for the) Petitioner

gned) ....Date...(Solicitor for the) Respondent

dress all communications for the Court to: The Chief Clerk, County Court* ....

....

to the Principal Registry, Somerset House, Strand, London WC2R 1LP) quoting the number in the top right-hand
ner of this form. This Court Office is open from 10 a.m. till 4 p.m. (4.30 p.m. at the Principal Registry) on Mondays
Fridays only.

YEZ The Solicitors' Law Stationery Society Ltd., Oyez House, 7 Spa Road, London SE16 3QQ

1991 Edition
12 91   F20570
5046930
• •

Divorce 109

8

IN THE LONDON COUNTY COURT   NUMBER:

BETWEEN: RENE MARKS   PETITIONER

                                        AND

                        JACK MARKS   RESPONDENT

RULE 2.63 QUESTIONNAIRE

THE PETITIONER REQUIRES ANSWERS TO THE FOLLOWING QUESTIONS
OF THE RESPONDENT:

1. What Bank accounts exist in the name of the Respondent
both in England and overseas and please exhibit associated
statement of the last six months regarding each of them.

2. What shares are owned by the Respondent and please
exhibit associated share certificates.

3. Please exhibit any pension policy held by the
Respondent with likely benefits accruing on any chosen
retirement date.

4. Please state the value of the home presently occupied
by the Respondent producing expert documentary evidence in
respect of it.

Signed.

Statement of Arrangements for Children
(Form M4, Appendix 1 FPR 1991)

FAMILY PROCEEDINGS RULES
Rule 2.2(2)

In the	County Court
Petitioner	
Respondent	
No. of Matter *(always quote this)*	

To the Petitioner

You must complete this form
if you or the respondent have any children ● under 16

or ● over 16 but under 18 if they are at school
or college or are training for a trade,
profession or vocation.

Please use black ink.

Please complete Parts I, II and III.

Before you issue a petition for divorce try to reach agreement with your husband/wife over the proposals for the children's future. There is space for him/her to sign at the end of this form if agreement is reached.

If your husband/wife does not agree with the proposals he/she will have the opportunity at a later stage to state why he/she does not agree and will be able to make his/her own proposals.

You should take or send the completed form, signed by you (and, if agreement is reached, by your husband/wife) together with a copy to the Court when you issue your petition.

Please refer to the explanatory notes issued regarding completion of the prayer of the petition if you are asking the Court to make any order regarding the children.

The Court will only make an order if it considers that an order will be better for the child(ren) than no order.

If you wish to apply for any of the orders which may be available to you under Part I or II of the Children Act 1989 you are advised to see a solicitor.

You should obtain legal advice from a solicitor or, alternatively, from an advice agency. The Law Society administers a national panel of solicitors to represent children and other parties involved in proceedings relating to children. Addresses of solicitors (including panel members) and advice agencies can be obtained from the Yellow Pages and the Solicitor's Regional Directory which can be found at Citizens' Advice Bureaux, Law Centres and any local library.

To the Respondent

The petitioner has completed Parts I, II and III of this form
which will be sent to the Court at the same time that the divorce petition is filed.

Please read all parts of the form carefully.

If you agree with the arrangements and proposals for the children you should sign Part IV of the form.

Please use black ink. You should return the form to the petitioner, or his/her solicitor.

If you do not agree with all or some of the arrangements or proposals you will be given the opportunity of saying so when the divorce petition is served on you.

1

9

Part I – Details of the children
Please read the instructions for boxes 1, 2 and 3 before you complete this section

---

1.   Children of both parties
(Give details only of any children born to you and the Respondent or adopted by you both)

	Forenames	Surname	Date of birth
(i)			
(ii)			
(iii)			
(iv)			
(v)			

---

2.   Other children of the family
(Give details of any other children treated by both of you as children of the family: for example your own or the Respondent's)

	Forenames	Surname	Date of birth	Relationship to Yourself	Respondent
(i)					
(ii)					
(iii)					
(iv)					
(v)					

---

3.   Other children who are not children of the family
(Give details of any children born to you or the Respondent that have not been treated as children of the family or adopted by you both)

	Forenames	Surname:	Date of birth
(i)			
(ii)			
(iii)			
(iv)			
(v)			

2

9

Part II – Arrangements for the children of the family
This part of the form must be completed. Give details for each child if arrangements are different.
If necessary, continue on another sheet and attach it to this form

4.	Home details *(Please tick the appropriate boxes)*	
	(a) The addresses at which the children now live	
	(b) Give details of the number of living rooms, bedrooms, etc. at the addresses in (a)	
	(c) Is the house rented or owned and by whom? Is the rent or any mortgage being regularly paid?	☐ No ☐ Yes
	(d) Give the names of all other persons living with the children including your husband/wife if he/she lives there. State their relationship to the children.	
	(e) Will there be any change in these arrangements?	☐ No ☐ Yes *(please give details)*

3

9

5.	Education and training details *(Please tick the appropriate boxes)*
(a) Give the names of the school, college or place of training attended by each child.	
(b) Do the children have any special educational needs?	☐ No ☐ Yes *(please give details)*
(c) Is the school, college or place of training, fee-paying?	☐ No ☐ Yes *(please give details of how much the fees are per term/year)*
Are fees being regularly paid?	☐ No ☐ Yes *(please give details)*
(d) Will there be any change in these arrangements?	☐ No ☐ Yes *(please give details)*

6.	**Childcare details** *(Please tick the appropriate boxes)*	
(a) Which parent looks after the children from day to day? If responsibility is shared, please give details.	
(b) Does that parent go out to work?	☐ No ☐ Yes *(please give details of his/her hours of work)*
(c) Does someone look after the children when the parent is not there?	☐ No ☐ Yes *(please give details)*
(d) Who looks after the children during school holidays?	
(e) Will there be any change in these arrangements?	☐ No ☐ Yes *(please give details)*

7.	**Maintenance** *(Please tick the appropriate boxes)*	
(a) Does your husband/wife pay towards the upkeep of the children? If there is another source of maintenance, please specify.	☐ No ☐ Yes *(please give details of how much)*
(b) Is the payment made under a court order?	☐ No ☐ Yes *(please give details, including the name of the court and case number)*
(c) Has maintenance for the children been agreed?	☐ No ☐ Yes
If not, will you be applying for a maintenance order for the children?	☐ No ☐ Yes *(please give details)*

9

8.	**Details for contact with the children** *(Please tick the appropriate boxes)*	
(a) Do the children see your husband/wife?	☐ No	☐ Yes *(please give details of how often and where)*
(b) Do the children ever stay with your husband/wife?	☐ No	☐ Yes *(please give details of how much)*
(c) Will there be any change to these arrangements? Please give details of the proposed arrangements for contact and residence.	☐ No	☐ Yes *(please give details of how much)*

9

9.	**Details of health** *(Please tick the appropriate boxes)*	
(a) Are the children generally in good health?	☐ Yes	☐ No *(please give details of any serious disability or chronic illness)*
(b) Do the children have any special health needs?	☐ No	☐ Yes *(please give details of the care needed and how it is to be provided)*

10.	**Details of care and other court proceedings** *(Please tick the appropriate boxes)*	
(a) Are the children in the care of a local authority, or under the supervision of a social worker or probation officer?	☐ No	☐ Yes *(please give details including any court proceedings)*
(b) Are any of the children on the Child Protection Register?	☐ No	☐ Yes *(please give details of the local authority and the date of registration)*
(c) Are there or have there been any proceedings in any Court involving the children, for example adoption, custody/residence, access/contact wardship, care, supervision or maintenance?	☐ No	☐ Yes *(please give details and send a copy of any order to the Court)*

7

9

Part III – To the Petitioner

Conciliation

If you and your husband/wife do not agree about the arrangements for the child(ren), would you agree to discuss the matter with a Conciliator and your husband/wife?

☐ No ☐ Yes

Declaration

I declare that the information I have given is correct and complete to the best of my knowledge.

Signed   (Petitioner)

Date:

Part IV – To the Respondent

I agree with the arrangements and proposals contained in Part I and II of this form.

Signed   (Respondent)

Date:

8

OYEZ The Solicitors' Law Stationery Society Ltd, Oyez House, 7 Spa Road, London SE16 3QQ

1991 Edition
6 92 F22621

Divorce 8

5046127
* * * *

10

OYEZ

Application for an Order
(Children Act 1989)

Form C1

The Court

To be completed by the Court

The full name(s) of the child(ren)

Date issued

Case number

Child(ren)'s number(s)

---

1. **About you (the Applicant).**
   State • *your title, full name, address, telephone number, date of birth and relationship to each child above*
   • *your solicitor's name, address, reference, telephone, fax and DX numbers.*

2. **The child(ren) and the order(s) you are applying for.**
   For each child state • *the full name, date of birth and sex*
   • *the type of order(s) you are applying for (for example, residence order, contact order, supervision order).*

1

[P.T.O.

10

3. **Other cases which concern the child(ren).**

   If there have ever been, or there are pending, any court cases which concern
   - *a child whose name you have put in paragraph 2*
   - *a full, half or step brother or sister of a child whose name you have put in paragraph 2*
   - *a person in this case who is or has been, involved in caring for a child whose name you have put in paragraph 2,*

   please attach a copy of the relevant order and give
   - *the name of the Court*
   - *the name and panel address (if known) of the guardian ad litem, if appointed*
   - *the name and contact address (if known) of the court welfare officer, if appointed*
   - *the name and contact address (if known) of the solicitor appointed for the child(ren).*

4. **The Respondent(s).**

   (Appendix 3 Family Proceedings Courts Rules 1991; Schedule 2 Family Proceedings (Children Act 1989) Rules 1991).

   For each Respondent state • *the title, full name and address*
   - *the date of birth (if known) or the age*
   - *the relationship to each child.*

2

10

5. Others to whom notice is to be given.

(Appendix 3 Family Proceedings Rules 1991; Schedule 2 Family Proceedings Courts (Children Act 1989) Rules 1991).

For each person state • *the title, full name and address*
                           • *the date of birth (if known) or age*
                           • *the relationship to each child.*

6. The care of the child(ren).

For each child in paragraph 2 state
• *the child's current address and how long the child has lived there*
• *whether it is the child's usual address and who cares for the child there*
• *the child's relationship to the other children (if any).*

7. Social Services.

For each child in paragraph 2 state
• *whether the child is known to the Social Services. If so, give the name of the social worker and the address of the Social Services Department*
• *whether the child is, or has been, on the Child Protection Register. If so, give the date of registration.*

[P.T.O.

10

8.   The education and health of the child(ren).

For each child state   • *the name of the school, college or place of training which the child attends*
• *whether the child is in good health. Give details of any serious disabilities or ill health*
• *whether the child has any special needs.*

9.   The Parent(s) of the child(ren).

For each child state   • *the full name of the child's mother and father*
• *whether the parents are, or have been, married to each other*
• *whether the parents live together. If so, where*
• *whether, to your knowledge, either of the parents have been involved in a Court case concerning a child. If so, give the date and the name of the Court.*

10.   The Family of the child(ren) (other children).

For any other child not already mentioned in the family (for example, a brother or a half sister) state
• *the full name and address*
• *the date of birth (if known) or age*
• *the relationship of the child to you.*

4

11. **Other adults.**

   State   • the full name, of any other adults (for example, lodgers) who live at the same address as any
                child named in paragraph 2
           • whether they live there all the time
           • whether, to your knowledge, the adult has been involved in a Court case concerning a child.
                If so, give the date and the name of the Court.

12. **Your reason(s) for applying and any plans for the child(ren).**

   State briefly your reasons for applying and what you want the Court to order.
           • *Do not* give a full statement if you are applying for an order under Section 8 of Children Act 1989.
                You may be asked to provide a full statement later.
           • *Do not* complete this section if this form is accompanied by a prescribed supplement.

13. **At the Court.**

   State   • whether you will need an interpreter at Court (parties are responsible for providing their own).
                If so, please specify the language
           • whether disabled facilities will be needed at Court.

Signed
(Applicant)   Date

OYEZ The Solicitors' Law Stationery Society Ltd, Oyez House, 7 Spa Road, London SE16 3QQ

1995 Edition
11.94 F28402
5037502
* * *

Children Act—C1

11

OYEZ

Supplement for an Application for Financial Provision for a Child or Variation of Financial Provision for a Child

Form C10

(Paragraph 4 Schedule 1 Children Act 1989)

The Court	To be completed by the Court
	Date issued
	Case number
The full name(s) of the child(ren)	Child(ren)'s number(s)

1. **About the application.**
   State whether you are seeking
   - *an order for a lump sum; a transfer of property; a settlement of property; periodical payments; secured periodical payments*

   or • *a variation of an order for periodical payments; secured periodical payments; payment of a lump sum by instalments.*

   Note: Applications concerning transfer of property, settlement of property or secured periodical payments can only be heard in the High Court or a County Court.

2. **Previous Court Orders and written agreements.**
   If a written agreement or Court Order has been made a copy should be attached to this application.
   If not available state • *the date*
   - *the terms*
   - *the parties*
   - *the Court.*

1

[P.T.O.

3. The Child Support Agency.

Assessment for maintenance

State whether the Agency has made an assessment for the maintenance of the child(ren):

☐ Yes ☐ No

If Yes, state whether you are applying for additional child maintenance

- *because the Child Support Agency will no longer deal with your claim. You should explain why the Agency will not deal with the claim*

or • *on top of payments made through the Child Support Agency. You should explain why you need additional maintenance and confirm that the Child Support Agency's assessment is the maximum amount obtainable.*

Written agreement for maintenance

State whether there is a written maintenance agreement: ☐ Yes ☐ No

If No, state whether you are applying for payment:

☐ for [a] stepchild[ren]

☐ in addition to child support maintenance already paid under a Child Support Agency assessment

　☐ to meet expenses arising from the disability of [a] child[ren]

　☐ to meet expenses incurred by [a] child[ren] in being educated or training for work

　☐ when either the child[ren] OR the person with care of the child[ren] OR the absent parent of the child[ren] is not habitually resident in the United Kingdom

　☐ for any other reason *(please specify):*

2

11

4.   About the Order.

State the terms of the Order you ask the Court to make and in particular

* *the amount you would like the Court to order*
* *whether you would like that amount paid weekly or monthly (if you are not applying for a lump sum)*
* *why you require the payments, or would like the Court to vary an existing order.*

5.   The collection of payment.

If payments are not to be collected and paid to you by the Child Support Agency, give full details of how you would like the payments collected. Possible ways are:

☐ **Directly to a bank, building society or post office account.**
Give the full name and address, sorting code and the number of the account into which payment is to be made.

☐ **By an attachment of earnings order.**
This is a Court order which is sent to the employer of the person who is to pay.

☐ **If you would like the Court to direct that money is paid in some other way.**
Please say what method you would like and if you do not mind how the money is paid, please say so. The Court will decide how it should be paid.

Signed   Date
(Applicant)

You should now complete a Statement of Means, Form Children Act — C10A

Case No	County Court

Between	_ _ _ _ _ _ _ _ _ _ _ _ _	Petitioner	Solicitor's ref.	_ _ _ _ _ _ _ _
and	_ _ _ _ _ _ _ _ _ _ _ _ _	Respondent	Solicitor's ref.	_ _ _ _ _ _ _ _

Financial Statement

Please fill in this form fully and accurately. You have a duty to the court to give a full, frank and clear disclosure of all your financial and other relevant circumstances.

A failure to give full and accurate disclosure may result in any order the court makes being set aside.

If you are found to have been deliberately untruthful, criminal proceedings for perjury may be taken against you.

You may annex documents to the form where they are specifically sought or are necessary to explain or clarify any of the information that you give.

If there is not enough room on the form for any particular piece of information, you may continue on an attached sheet of paper.

I _

the above named [Petitioner]
of

make oath and confirm that the information given on the following pages is a full, frank, clear and accurate disclosure of my financial and other relevant circumstances.

Form E
Quantum Skip (version 1) from Class Publishing

12

Part 1 General Information

1.1 Full Name

1.2 Date of Birth

Date	Month	Year

1.3 Date of Marriage

Date	Month	Year

1.4 Occupation

1.5 Date of the separation

Date	Month	Year

Tick here ☐ if not applicable

1.6 Date of the:

Petition			Decree Nisi/Decree of Judicial Separation			Decree Absolute		
Date	Month	Year	Date	Month	Year	Date	Month	Year

1.7 If you have remarried, or will remarry, state the date

Date	Month	Year

1.8 Do you live with another person? ☐ Yes ☐ No

1.9 Do you intend to live with someone within the next six months? ☐ Yes ☐ No

1.10 Details of any children of the family

Full names	Date of Birth			With whom does the child live?
	Date	Month	Year	

1.11 Give details of the state of health of yourself and the children

Yourself	Children

1.12 Give details of the present and proposed future educational arrangements for the children.

Present arrangements	Future arrangements

1.13 Give details of any Child Support Maintenance Assessments or Child Maintenance Orders made between the parties. If no assessment or agreement has been made, give an estimate of the liability of the non-residential parent under the Child Support Act 1991, in respect of the children of the family.

1.14 If this application is to vary an order, give details of the order that is to be varied and attach a copy of the order. Give the reasons for asking for the order to be varied.

1.15 Give details of any other court cases between you and your husband/wife, whether in relation to money, property, children or anything else.

Case No.	Court

1.16 Specify your present residence and the occupants of it and on what terms you occupy it (e.g. tenant, owner-occupier).

Address	Occupants	Terms of occupation

12

Part 2 Financial Details   *Capital: Realisable Assets*

* If you have obtained a valuation within the last six months attach a copy. If not, give your own estimate of the property value. A copy of your most recent mortgage statement is also required.

2.1 Give details of your interest in the matrimonial home.

Property name and address	Land Registry Title No.	Nature and extent of your interest	*Property value

Mortgagee's Name and address	Type of mortgage	Balance outstanding on any mortgage	Total current value of your beneficial interest
1st			
2nd			
Other:			

NET value of your interest in the matrimonial home (A)   £

2.2 Give details of all other properties, land, and buildings in which you have an interest.

Property name(s) and address(es)	Land Registry Title No.	Nature and extent of your interest	*Property value
1.			
2.			
3.			

Mortgagee's Name(s) and address(es)	Type of mortgage	Balance outstanding on any mortgage	Total current value of your interest
1.			
2.			
3.			

TOTAL value of the above
(not including the matrimonial home)   (B1)   £

12

2.3 Give details of all bank, building society, and National Savings accounts, in credit, which you hold or have an interest in. Include all PEPs, TESSAs and ISAs. For joint accounts, give your interest and the name of the account holder. If the account is overdrawn, include in Liabilities section at 2.12
You must attach your bank statements covering the last 12 months for each account listed

Name of bank or building society including Branch name	Type of account (e.g. current)	Account number	Name of other account holder *(if applicable)*	Balance at the date of this Statement	Total current value of your interest
1.					
2.					
3.					
4.					
5.					
TOTAL value of your interest in ALL accounts					(B2) £

2.4 Give details of all stocks, gilts and other quoted securities which you hold or have an interest in. Do not include dividend income as this will be dealt with separately later on.

Name	Type	Size	Current value	Total current value of your interest
TOTAL value of your interest in ALL holdings				(B3) £

2.5 Give details of all life insurance policies which you hold or in which you have an interest, including those that do not have a surrender value, for each policy.

Policy details including name of company, policy type and number	If policy is charged, state in whose favour and amount of charge	Maturity date			Surrender Value	Total current value of your interest
		Date	Month	Year		

You must attach any surrender value quotations   TOTAL value of your interest in ALL policies   (B4) £

12

2.6 Give details of all issues of National Savings Certificates which you hold or have an interest in.

Name of issue	Nominal amount	Current value	Total current value of your interest
		TOTAL value of ALL your certificates	(B5) £

2.7 Give details of all of National Savings Bonds (including Premium Bonds) and other bonds which you hold or have an interest in.

Type of Bond	Bond holder's number	Current value	Total current value of your interest
		TOTAL value of ALL your bonds	(B6) £

2.8 Give details of all monies which are OWED TO YOU. Include sums owed in director's or partnership accounts.

Brief description of debt	Balance outstanding	Total current value of your interest
	TOTAL value of your interest in ALL debts owed to you	(B7) £

2.9 Give details of all of cash savings held in excess of £300. You must state where it is held and the currency it is held in.

Where held	Amount	Currency	Total current value of your interest

TOTAL value of ALL your cash   (B8) £

2.10 Give details of personal belongings individually worth more than £500.
(Include cars (gross value), collections, pictures, jewellery, furniture, and household belongings (this list is not exhaustive).

Item	Sale value	Total estimated current value of your interest

TOTAL value of your interest in ALL personal belongings   (B9) £

.11 Give details of any other realisable assets not yet mentioned, for example, unit trusts, investment trusts, commodities, business expansion schemes and futures (this list is not exhaustive).
This is where you must mention any other realisable assets.

Type	Current value	Total current value of your interest

TOTAL value of your interest in ALL other realisable assets   (B10) £

Now add together all the figures in the previous total boxes (B1 to B10) to give the TOTAL current value of ALL your interest in realisable assets.

(B) £

12

Part 2 Financial Details   *Capital: Liabilities*

2.12 Give details of any liabilities you have. **Exclude** mortgages on property dealt with above. **Include** money owed on credit cards and store cards, bank loans, hire purchase agreements and any overdrawn bank or building society accounts.

Liability (i.e. total, amount owed, current monthly payments and term of loan/debt)	Current amount	Total current value of your share of the liability
TOTAL value of ALL your liabilities		(C1) £

Part 2 Financial Details   *Capital: Capital Gains Tax*

2.13 If any Capital Gains Tax would be payable on the disposal now of any of your realisable assets, give your estimate of the tax.

Asset	Capital Gains Tax	Total current value of your liability
TOTAL value of ALL your Capital Gains Tax liabilities		(C2) £

Now add together C1 + C2 to give:-
TOTAL net value of your liabilities   **(C)**   £

Now take the liabilities total from the realisable assets total (A+B-C), to give:-   **(D)**   £
TOTAL net value of your personal assets

Part 2 Financial Details   *Capital: Business Assets*

2.14 Give details of all your business interests.   *You must attach a copy of the last 2 years accounts and any other document on which you base your valuation.*

Name and nature of your business	Your ESTIMATE of the current value of your interest	Your ESTIMATE of any possible Capital Gains Tax payable on disposal	Basis of valuation *(No formal valuation is required at this time)*	What is the extent of your interest?	Total net current value of your interest

TOTAL current value of your interest in business assets   **(E)**

15 List any directorships you hold or held in the last 12 months

12

FINANCIAL STATEMENT
[Applicant] *[Respondent]*

In the · · · · · · · ·

*[County Court]
*[Principal Registry of the Family Division]

Case No.
Always quote this

*[delete as appropriate]

Between Applicant

and

Respondent

Solicitor's Ref:

Solicitor's Ref:

Please fill in this form fully and accurately. Where any box is not applicable write "N/A". You have a duty to the court to give a full, frank and clear disclosure of all your financial and other relevant circumstances.

A failure to give full and accurate disclosure may result in any order the court makes being set aside.

If you are found to have been deliberately untruthful, criminal proceedings for perjury may be taken against you.

You must attach documents to the form where they are specifically sought and you may attach other documents where it is necessary to explain or clarify any of the information that you give.

Essential documents, which **must** accompany this Statement, are detailed at questions 2.1, 2.2, 2.3, 2.5, 2.14, 2.18 and 2.20.

If there is not enough room on the form for any particular piece of information, you may continue on an attached sheet of paper.

This statement must be sworn before an Officer of the Court
or a Commissioner for Oaths
before it is filed with the Court
or sent to the other party
(see page 20).

Form E Financial Statement

Glossary of Legal Terms

Acknowledgement of Service The form that is sent with the petition for the respondent to acknowledge the petition's receipt. When the form is returned, service is accepted as having been achieved.

Affidavit A written statement, made on oath, containing a version of events, beliefs and opinions which will be relied upon as evidence by the person making the affidavit.

Ancillary Relief Long-term maintenance which comes into effect after decree absolute.

Answer The reply to a divorce petition or cross-petition.

Application All divorce proceedings and court orders begin with an application: standard forms to do this are available from the court office.

Calderbank Letter A letter containing a financial offer, written in advance of a final hearing (see p.44).

In Chambers Almost all divorce proceedings are heard in chambers, in other words in private.

Child of the Family A child who naturally belongs to the husband and wife who are getting divorced, or any other child who has been treated by the two of them as a child of the family.

Clean Break An agreement that the two people who are divorcing will have no further financial dependence on each other.

Conciliation An attempt to obtain agreement between the divorcing couple concerning their children and any other areas of conflict.

Contact Formerly called access, contact is the visiting right or staying right of either parent to a child of the family; in other words, a right to have contact with that child.

Co-respondent The person with whom it is alleged the respondent has committed adultery.

Cross-petition The reasons for the breakdown of the marriage put forward by the respondent, which will differ from those stated by the petitioner.

Decree Absolute The final order of the court to dissolve the marriage.

Decree Nisi The provisional order of the court to dissolve the marriage.

Domicile A person's permanent home.

Equity The net proceeds of the sale of the family home, after deduction of estate agent's and solicitor's fees and paying off the remaining mortgage.

Habitual Residence The place where a person resides 'as of habit' – that is, permanently.

Injunction A court order to restrain or prevent the recipient from, for example, molesting his wife or entering the family home.

Jurisdiction A court's authority and the geographical area covered by that authority.

Legal Aid Payment by the state for legal representation; certain conditions are attached to its availability (see p.67).

Nullity A decree stating that a marriage is null and void.

Prohibited Steps Order An order restricting what a parent may do with a child – preventing the parent, for instance, from taking the child out of the country.

Reply A response/defence filed by the petitioner in answer to the reply and/or cross-petition of the respondent.

Residency Formerly known as custody, this refers to a parent having the child of the family permanently with him/her – in other words he or she has the permanent residency of the child. Residency can also be shared, for which purpose an order of shared residency can be made.

Service The manner in which the parties to the divorce receive the necessary court forms.

Index